Fodor's  Pocket Acapulco

Including Taxco, Ixtapa and Zihuatanejo

Parts of this book appear in *Fodor's Mexico*

Fodor's Travel Publications, Inc.
New York • Toronto • London •
Sydney • Auckland

Fodor's Acapulco

Editors: Hannah Borgeson, Anto Howard, Edie Jarolim
Contributors: Steven Amsterdam, Wendy Luft, Erica Meltzer, Tracy Patruno, Craig Vetter
Creative Director: Fabrizio La Rocca
Cartographer: David Lindroth
Illustrator: Karl Tanner
Cover Photograph: Peter Guttman
Design: Vignelli Associates

Special Sales

Fodor's Travel Publications are available at special discounts for sales promotions or premiums. Special editions, including personalized covers, excerpts of existing guides, and corporate imprints, can be created in large quantities for special needs. For more information, contact your local bookseller or write to Special Markets, Fodor's Travel Publications, 201 E. 50th St., New York, NY 10022; Random House of Canada, Ltd., Marketing Dept., 1265 Aerowood Dr., Mississauga, Ontario L4W 1B9; Fodor's Travel Publications, 20 Vauxhall Bridge Rd., London SW1V 2SA.

Contents

Contents

Foreword

"Nirvana by the Sea," "Miami on the Pacific," and "Queen of the Mexican Resorts" are among the names that have, at one time or another, been applied to Acapulco, the archetypal beachgoer's destination. Legendary haven for the jet-set, politicians, and literary greats, Acapulco today attracts those of more modest means seeking almost-guaranteed sunshine; bargains in silver, leather, and Mexican handicrafts; and the frenzied nightlife of lore.

Three and a half hours up the coast, the newer resort towns of Ixtapa and Zihuatenejo offer equally splendid sun and sand, far cleaner bays, and even better prices. The pace of the nightlife can't compare with the year-round party in Acapulco, but travelers in search of beauty and serenity will find it up here, and the two towns offer lodging, dining, and shopping of a sophistication to rival Acapulco's.

The sliding peso and the so-called Mexican Riviera's proximity to the United States make these resorts even more attractive as a vacation option to those north of the border, especially in winter. This guide presents the widest range of sights, activities, restaurants, and accommodations and, within that range, selections that are worthwhile and of the best value. The descriptions provided are just enough for you to make your own informed choices from among our selections.

While every care has been taken to ensure the accuracy of the information in this guide, the passage of time will always bring change and, consequently, the publisher cannot accept responsibility for errors that may occur.

All prices and opening times quoted here are based on information supplied to us at press time. Hours and admission fees may change, however, and the prudent traveler will avoid inconvenience by calling ahead.

Fodor's wants to hear about your travel experiences, both pleasant and unpleasant. When a hotel or restaurant fails to live up to its billing, let us know and we will investigate the complaint and revise our entries where the facts warrant it.

Send your letters to the editors of Fodor's Travel Publications, 201 East 50th Street, New York, N Y 10022.

Introduction

By Anya Schiffrin

Updated by Wendy Luft

For sun lovers, beach bums, and other hedonists, Acapulco is the ideal holiday resort. Don't expect high culture, historic monuments, or haute cuisine. Anyone who ventures to this Pacific resort 433 kilometers (260 miles) south of Mexico City does so to relax. Translate that as swimming, shopping, and going out at night. Everything takes place against a staggeringly beautiful natural backdrop: Acapulco Bay is one of the world's best natural harbors, and it is the city's centerpiece. By day the deep blue water looks clean and tempting; at night it flashes and sparkles with the city lights.

The weather is Acapulco's major draw—warm waters, almost constant sunshine, and year-round temperatures in the 80s. It comes as no surprise, then, that most people plan their day around lying on their towel on some part of Acapulco's many miles of beach. Tame and wild water sport options abound—everything from waterskiing to snorkeling, diving, and parasailing. Motorboat rides and fishing trips are less strenuous possibilities. Championship golf courses, tennis courts, and the food and crafts markets also occasionally lure some visitors away from the beach, but not out of the sun.

Most people rouse themselves from their hammocks, deck chairs, or towels only when it is feeding time, and eating is one of Acapulco's great pleasures. In addition to the glitzy places, there are many good no-frills, down-home Mexican restaurants. These spots give you a glimpse into the real Mexico: office workers breaking for lunch, groups of men socializing over a cup of coffee.

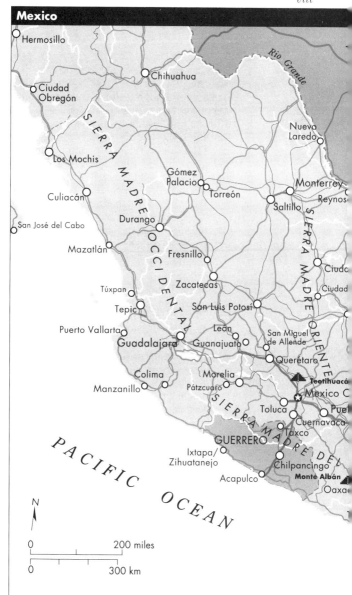

Mexico

Hermosillo

Ciudad Obregón

Chihuahua

Los Mochis

Culiacán

San José del Cabo

SIERRA MADRE OCCIDENTAL

Gómez Palacio

Torreón

Durango

Mazatlán

Fresnillo

Zacatecas

Túxpan

Tepic

Puerto Vallarta

San Luis Potosí

León

Guadalajara

Guanajuato

San Miguel de Allende

Colima

Morelia

Querétaro

Manzanillo

Pátzcuaro

SIERRA MADRE DEL

Toluca

Mexico C

Teotihuacá

Cuernavaca

Puel

Taxco

GUERRERO

Ixtapa/ Zihuatanejo

Chilpancingo

Monte Albán

Acapulco

Oaxa

Nueva Laredo

Monterrey

Reynos

Saltillo

SIERRA MADRE ORIENTE

Ciuda

Ciudad

Río Grande

PACIFIC OCEAN

N

0   200 miles

0   300 km

EXAS

MISS.

ALA.

LOUISIANA

Brownsville

Matamoros

Gulf of Mexico

d Victoria

Mante

ampico

Poza Rica

El Tajín

Veracruz

ity

la

Mérida

Tizimin

Cancún

Chichén Itzá

Uxmal

Campeche

Cozumel

Cobá

Xel-Há

Y U C A T A N

Tulum

Isla Mujeres

Bahía de Campeche

Ciudad del Carmen

Coatzacoalcos

Chetumal

Caribbean Sea

Minatitlán

Villahermosa

SUR

ca

Palenque

Tuxtla Gutiérrez

San Cristóbal de las Casas

BELIZE

ehuantepec

Huatulco

Comitán

Golfo de Tehuantepec

GUATEMALA

HONDURAS

Tapachula

At night Acapulco is transformed as the city rouses itself from the day's torpor and prepares for the long hours ahead. Even though Acapulco's heyday is past, its nightlife is legendary, despite the fact that many of the discos along the main drag still look as if they were designed in the early '70s by an architect who bought mirrors and strobe lights wholesale. Perpetually crowded, the discos are grouped in twos and threes, so most people go to several places in one night.

Acapulco was originally an important port for the Spanish, who used it to trade with countries in the Far East. The Spanish built Fuerte de San Diego (Fort San Diego) to protect the city from pirates, and today the fort houses a historical museum. The name of the late Teddy Stauffer, an entrepreneurial Swiss, is practically synonymous with that of modern Acapulco. He hired the first cliff divers at La Quebrada in Old Acapulco and founded the Boom Boom Room, the town's first dance hall, and Tequila A Go-Go, its first discotheque. The Hotel Mirador at La Quebrada and the area stretching from Caleta to Hornos beaches, near today's Old Acapulco, were the center of activity in the 1950s, when Acapulco was a town of 20,000 with an economy based largely on fishing.

Former President Miguel Alemán Valdés bought up miles of the coast just before the road and the airport were built. The Avenida Costera Miguel Alemán bears his name today. Since the late 1940s, Acapulco has expanded eastward so that today it is one of Mexico's largest cities, with a population of approximately 2 million. Currently under development are a 3,000-acre expanse known as Acapulco Diamante and the areas known as Punta Diamante and Playa Diamante.

1   Essential Information

Before You Go

Government Information Offices

Tourist Information
The **State of Guerrero Department of Tourism (SEFOTUR**; Costera Miguel Alemán 187, across from Bodegas Aurrerá, tel. 74/86–91–64 or 74/84–31–40) is open Monday–Friday 9–2 and 4–7. The staff speaks English, has brochures and maps on other parts of Mexico, and can help you find a hotel room. **Mexico Surface Tourism Office for U.S. and Canada** (2707 N. Loop W, Suite 440, Houston, TX 77008, tel. 713/880–8772, fax 713/880–0286).

For a current calendar of events, train schedules and fares, brochures and other general information about travel in Mexico, contact the nearest **Mexican Government Tourism Office.**

In the U.S.
405 Park Avenue, Suite 1401, New York, NY 10022, tel. 212/755–7261, fax 212/753–2874; 1911 Pennsylvania Avenue NW, Washington, DC 20006, tel. 202/728–1750, fax 202/728–1758; 128 Aragon Avenue, Coral Gables, FL 33134, tel. 305/443–9160, fax 305/443–1186; 70 E. Lake Street, Suite 1413, Chicago, IL 60601, tel. 312/606–9015, fax 312/606-9012; 2707 N. Loop W, Suite 450, Houston, TX 77008, tel. 713/880–5153, fax 713/880–1833; 10100 Santa Monica Boulevard, Suite 224, Los Angeles, CA 90067, tel. 310/203–8191, fax 310/203–8316. If there is no office near you, call 800/446–3942.

In Canada
1 Place Ville Marie, Suite 1526, Montreal, Quebec H3B 2B5, tel. 514/871–1052, fax 514/871-3825; 2 Bloor Street W, Suite 1801, Toronto, Ontario M4W 3E2, tel. 416/925–0704, fax 416/925-6061; 1610–999 W. Hastings St., Vancouver, BC, V6C 2W2, tel. 604/669–2845, fax 604/669–3498.

When to Go

The weather in Acapulco is basically the same all year, with an average temperature of 80°F (or 27°C). The hottest months are June, July, and August; the coolest is January. During high season, December 15 to Easter, it rarely rains. The summer is more humid, August and October being the rainiest months. Whatever the time of year, the water is always warm. Low season (July to October) offers the advantage of lower prices and fewer people, though some restaurants and hotels close for vacation or to make repairs.

November is considered a "shoulder" month; prices will be midway between those in effect in high and low seasons. But even in low season, tour operators fill up the biggest hotels. The peak time for crowds is December 25 to January 3, when you may have trouble booking a hotel room. *Semana Santa*, the week before Easter, is very popular with Mexicans; schools are in recess and families come to Acapulco for their children's vacation. Budget hotels get very noisy and many tourists party all night and sleep on the beaches. Remember, no matter when you want to visit, book ahead to avoid disappointment.

Climate   The following are the average daily maximum and minimum temperatures for Acapulco.

Jan.	88F	31C	**May**	90F	32C	**Sept.**	90F	32C
	72	22		77	25		77	25
Feb.	88F	31C	**June**	90F	32C	**Oct.**	90F	32C
	72	22		77	25		77	25
Mar.	88F	31C	**July**	91F	33C	**Nov.**	90F	32C
	72	22		77	25		75	24
Apr.	88F	31C	**Aug.**	91F	33C	**Dec.**	88F	31C
	72	22		77	25		73	23

Information Sources   For current weather conditions and forecasts for cities in the United States and abroad, plus the local time and helpful travel tips, call the **Weather Channel Connection** (tel. 900/932–8437; 95¢ per minute) from a touch-tone phone.

Festivals and Seasonal Events   Mexico has a full calendar of national holidays, saints' days, and special events; below are some of the most important or unusual ones. For further information and exact dates, contact the Mexican Government Tourism Office (*see* Government Information Offices, *above*).

Jan. 1: New Year's Day is a major celebration throughout Mexico. Agricultural and livestock fairs are held in the provinces.

Jan. 6: Feast of Epiphany is the day the Three Kings bring gifts to Mexican children.

Jan. 17: Feast of San Antonio Abad honors animals all over Mexico. Household pets and livestock alike are decked out with flowers and ribbons and taken to a nearby church for a blessing.

Feb. 2: Día de la Candelaria, or Candlemas Day, means fiestas, parades, bullfights, and lantern-decorated streets.

Feb.–Mar.: Carnaval is celebrated throughout Mexico with colorful parades and fiestas.

Mar. 21: Benito Juárez's Birthday is a national holiday.

Mar.–Apr.: Holy Week (*Semana Santa*) is observed with special passion plays during this week leading up to Easter Sunday.

May 1: Labor Day is a day for workers to parade through the streets.

May 5: Cinco de Mayo marks the anniversary of the French defeat by Mexican troops in Puebla in 1862.

May 15: Feast of San Isidro Labrador is celebrated nationwide with the blessing of new seeds and animals.

June 1: Navy Day is commemorated in all Mexican seaports and is especially colorful in Acapulco.

June 24: Saint John the Baptist Day is a popular national holiday, with many Mexicans observing a tradition of tossing a "blessing" of water on most anyone within reach.

July 16: Our Lady of Mt. Carmel Day is a celebration with fairs, bullfights, fireworks, sporting competitions, and even a major fishing tournament.

Late July: Feast of Santiago is a national holiday that features *charreadas*, Mexican-style rodeos.

Aug. 15: Feast of the Assumption of the Blessed Virgin Mary is celebrated nationwide with religious processions.

Sept. 15–16: Independence Day is when all of Mexico celebrates independence with fireworks and parties that outblast New Year's Eve.

Oct. 4: Feast of St. Francis of Assisi is a day for processions dedicated to St. Francis.

Oct. 12: Columbus Day is a national holiday in Mexico.

Nov. 2: All Souls' Day, or **Day of the Dead,** is when Mexicans remember the departed in a merry way, with candy skulls sold on street corners and picnickers spreading blankets in cemeteries.

Nov. 20: Anniversary of the Mexican Revolution is a national holiday.

Nov.–Dec.: National Silver Fair is an annual Taxco event during which silver is exhibited and sold.

Dec. 12: Feast Day of the Virgin of Guadalupe is the day on which Mexico's patron saint is feted with processions and native folk dances.

Dec. 16–25: The Posadas and **Christmas** are when candlelight processions lead to Christmas parties and to *piñatas* (suspended paper animals or figurines) that are broken open to yield gifts.

What to Pack

Pack light: Though baggage carts are available now at airports, luggage restrictions on international flights are tight, and you'll want to save space for purchases.

Clothing Acapulco is both casual and elegant; you'll see high-style designer sportswear, tie-dyed T-shirts, cotton slacks and walking shorts, and plenty of colorful sundresses. Bring lightweight sports clothes, bathing suits, and cover-ups for the beach. The sun can be fierce; bring a sun hat (or buy one locally) and sunscreen for the beach and for sightseeing. Bathing suits and immodest clothing are inappropriate for shopping and sightseeing. You'll need a sweater or jacket to cope with hotel and restaurant air-conditioning, which can be glacial. Few restaurants require jacket and tie.

Miscellaneous Bring as much film as you're allowed, because film is expensive in Mexico. Also pack a spare pair of sunglasses, plenty of sunblock, a small flashlight, insect repellent, and a plastic water bottle for carrying your own supply on the road. Bring an extra pair of eyeglasses or contact lenses in your carry-on luggage. If you have a health problem that requires a prescription drug, pack enough to last the duration of the trip or have your doctor write a prescription using the drug's generic name, because brand names vary from country to country. Always carry prescription drugs in their original packaging to avoid problems with customs officials. Don't pack medication in luggage that you plan to check. Pack a list of the offices that supply refunds for lost or stolen traveler's checks.

Electricity Electrical converters are not necessary because the country operates on the 60-cycle, 120-volt system; however, many Mexican outlets have not been updated to accommodate three-prong and polarized plugs (those with one larger prong), so you may need an adapter.

Luggage Free airline baggage allowances depend on the
Regulations airline, the route, and the class of your ticket; ask in advance. In general, on domestic flights and on international flights between the United States and foreign destinations, you are entitled to check two bags—neither exceeding 62 inches, or 158 centimeters (length + width + height), or weighing more than 70 pounds (32 kilograms). A third piece may be brought aboard; its total dimensions are generally limited to less than 45 inches (114 centimeters), so it will fit easily under the seat in front of you or in the overhead compartment. There are variations, so ask in advance. In the United States, the Federal Aviation Administration (FAA) gives airlines broad latitude to limit carry-on allowances and tailor them to different aircraft and operational conditions. Charges for excess, oversize, or overweight pieces vary.

If you are flying between two foreign destinations, note that baggage allowances may be determined not by piece but by weight—generally 88 pounds (40 kilograms) of luggage in first class, 66 pounds (30 kilograms) in business class, and 44 pounds (20 kilograms) in economy. If your flight between two cities abroad *connects* with your transatlantic or transpacific flight, the piece method still applies.

Safeguarding Before leaving home, itemize your bags' con-
Your Luggage tents and their worth in case they go astray. To minimize that risk, tag them inside and out with your name, address, and phone number. (If you use your home address, cover it so that potential thieves can't see it.) Put a copy of your itinerary inside each bag so that you can easily be tracked.

At check-in, make sure that the tag attached by baggage handlers bears the correct three-letter code for your destination. If your bags do not arrive with you, or if you detect damage, file a written report with the airline before you leave the airport.

Getting Money from Home

Cash Machines Many automated-teller machines (ATMs) are tied to international networks such as **Cirrus** and **Plus**. You can use your bank card at ATMs away from home to withdraw money from an account and get cash advances on a credit-card account if your card has been programmed with a personal identification number, or PIN. Check in advance on limits on withdrawals and cash advances within specified periods. Ask whether your bank-card or credit-card PIN will need to be reprogrammed for use in the area you'll be visiting. Four digits are commonly used overseas. Note that Discover gives cash advances only in the United States. On cash advances you are charged interest from the day you receive the money from ATMs as well as from tellers. Although transaction fees for ATM withdrawals abroad may be higher than fees for withdrawals at home, Cirrus and Plus exchange rates are excellent, because they are based on wholesale rates offered only by major banks.

Plan ahead: Obtain ATM locations and the names of affiliated cash-machine networks before departure. For specific foreign Cirrus locations, call 800/424–7787; for foreign Plus locations, consult the Plus directory at your local bank.

Wiring Money You don't have to be a cardholder to send or receive a **MoneyGram from American Express** for up to $10,000. Go to a MoneyGram agent (in retail and convenience stores and American Express travel offices), and pay up to $1,000 with a credit card and anything over that in cash. You are allowed a free long-distance call to give the transaction code to your intended recipient, who need only present identification and the reference number to the nearest MoneyGram agent to pick up the cash. MoneyGram agents are in more than 70 countries (tel. 800/926–9400 for locations). Fees range from 3% to 10%, depending on the amount and method of payment.

You can also use **Western Union.** To wire money, take either cash or a cashier's check to the nearest office or call and use your MasterCard or Visa. Money sent from the United States or Canada will be available for pickup at agent locations in 78 countries within minutes. Once the money is in the system, it can be picked up at any one of 22,000 locations (call 800/325–6000 for the one nearest you).

Mexican Currency

As of January 1, 1993, the unit of currency in Mexico became the *nuevo peso*, or new peso, which is subdivided into 100 centavos. At press time (March 1994) one U.S. dollar was equal to 3.04 nuevo pesos, one Canadian dollar was equal to 2.33 pesos, and a pound sterling equaled 4.7 pesos. The old peso, which had a cumbersome exchange of 3,000 to one U.S. dollar, was to be completely phased out by January 1994, but at press time there was still old currency in circulation, and many public phones and vending machines still accepted only the old coins. The new paper currency is the same color as the old and comes in denominations of 10, 20, 50, and 100, equal to the old 10,000, 20,000, 50,000 and 100,000 notes, respectively. Newly introduced were the 2-, 5-, 10-, and 20-peso coins. The 1,000-, 500-, 200-, 100-, and 50-peso coins were replaced by the smaller, newly designed 1-peso and 50-, 20-, 10-, and 5-centavo coins. Needless to say, it is somewhat confusing. Travelers should examine coins carefully before paying and when receiving change. Note: NP$ generally precedes prices in new pesos. To avoid fraud, it's wise to make sure that "NP" is clearly marked on all credit-card receipts.

Dollars are widely accepted in many parts of Mexico. Many tourist shops and market vendors, as well as virtually all hotel service personnel, take them, too.

What It Will Cost

Mexico has a reputation for being inexpensive, particularly compared with other North American vacation spots such as the Caribbean islands. Actual costs will vary with the when, where, and how of your travel in Mexico. "When" is discussed in When to Go, *above.* As to "how," tourists seeking a destination as much as possible like home, who travel only by air or package tour, stay at international hotel chain properties, eat at restaurants catering to tourists, and shop at fixed-price tourist-oriented malls may not find Mexico such a bargain. Anyone who wants a closer look at the country and is not wedded to standardized creature comforts can spend as little as $35 a day on room, board, and local transportation. Speaking Spanish is also helpful in bargaining situations and when asking for dining recommendations. As a rule, the less English is spoken, the cheaper things will be (*see also* Language, *below*).

Acapulco is one of the more expensive places to visit in Mexico. Taxis are supposed to charge fixed rates to and from the airport and between hotels and beaches or downtown, but be sure to agree upon a price before getting in. Water sports can cost as much as they do on the Caribbean islands. All the beach towns, however, offer budget accommodations, and the smaller, less accessible ones are often more moderately priced.

Taxes Mexico has a value-added tax of 10% called I.V.A. (*impuesto de valor agregado*), which is occasionally (and illegally) waived for cash purchases. Other taxes and charges apply for phone calls, dining, and lodging. An airport departure tax of U.S. $11.50 or the peso equivalent must be paid at the airport for international flights from Mexico, and there is a domestic air departure tax of U.S. $8.40. Traveler's checks and credit cards are not accepted.

Passports and Visas

If your passport is lost or stolen abroad, report the loss immediately to the nearest embassy or consulate and to the local police. If you can provide the consular officer with the information contained in the passport, he or she will usually be able to issue you a new passport promptly. For this reason, keep a photocopy of the data page of your passport separate from your money and traveler's checks. Also leave a photocopy with a relative or friend at home.

U.S. Citizens All U.S. citizens need a valid passport to enter Mexico for stays of more than 180 days. You can pick up new and renewal application forms at any of the 13 U.S. Passport Agency offices and at some post offices and courthouses. Although passports are usually mailed within four weeks of your application's receipt, allow five weeks or more from April through summer. Call the Department of State Office of Passport Services' information line (tel. 202/647–0518) for fees, documentation requirements, and other details.

Canadian Citizens Canadian citizens need a valid passport to enter Mexico for stays of more than 180 days. Application forms are available at 23 regional passport offices as well as at post offices and travel agencies. Whether for a first or a subsequent passport, you must apply in person. Children under 16 may be included on a parent's passport but must have their own to travel alone. Passports are valid for five years and are usually mailed within two weeks of an application's receipt. For fees, documentation requirements, and other information in English or French, call the passport office (tel. 514/283–2152 or 800/567–6868).

Customs and Duties

On Arrival Upon entering Mexico, you will be given a baggage declaration form and asked to itemize what you're bringing into the country. You are allowed to bring in two liters of spirits or wine for personal use; 400 cigarettes, 50 cigars, or 250 grams of tobacco; a reasonable amount of perfume for personal use; one movie camera and one regular camera and 12 rolls of film for each; and gift items not to exceed a total of $300. You are not allowed to bring meat, vegetables, plants, fruit, or flowers into the country.

Returning Home If you are bringing any foreign-made equipment into Mexico, such as cameras, it's wise to carry the original receipt with you or register the equipment at the airport with U.S. Customs before you depart (Form 4457). Otherwise you may end up paying duty on your return.

U.S. Customs   If you've been out of the country for at least 48 hours and haven't already used the exemption, or any part of it, in the past 30 days, you may bring home $400 worth of foreign goods duty-free. So can each member of your family, regardless of age; and your exemptions may be pooled, so one of you can bring in more if another brings in less. A flat 10% duty applies to the next $1,000 worth of goods; above $1,400, the rate varies with the merchandise. (If the 48-hour or 30-day limits apply, your duty-free allowance drops to $25, which may not be pooled.)

Travelers 21 or older may bring back 1 liter of alcohol duty-free, provided the beverage laws of the state through which they reenter the United States allow it. In addition, 100 non-Cuban cigars and 200 cigarettes are allowed, regardless of your age. Antiques and works of art more than 100 years old are duty-free.

Gifts valued at less than $50 may be mailed to the U.S. duty-free, with a limit of one package per day per addressee, and do not count as part of your exemption (do not send alcohol or tobacco products or perfume valued at more than $5); mark the package "Unsolicited Gift" and write the nature of the gift and its retail value on the outside. Most reputable stores will handle the mailing for you.

For a copy of "Know Before You Go," a free brochure detailing what you may and may not bring back to the United States, rates of duty, and other pointers, contact the **U.S. Customs Service** (Box 7407, Washington, DC 20044, tel. 202/927–6724).

Canadian   Once per calendar year, when you've been out of
Customs   Canada for at least seven days, you may bring in C$300 worth of goods duty-free. If you've been away less than seven days but more than 48 hours, the duty-free exemption drops to C$100 but can be claimed any number of times (as can a C$20 duty-free exemption for absences of 24 hours or more). You cannot combine the yearly and 48-hour exemptions, use the C$300 exemption only partially (to save the balance for a later trip), or pool exemptions with family members. Goods claimed under the C$300 exemption may

follow you by mail; those claimed under the lesser exemptions must accompany you.

Alcohol and tobacco products may be included in the yearly and 48-hour exemptions but not in the 24-hour exemption. If you meet the age requirements of the province through which you reenter Canada, you may bring in, duty-free, 1.14 liters (40 imperial ounces) of wine or liquor *or* two dozen 12-ounce cans or bottles of beer or ale. If you are 16 or older, you may bring in, duty-free, 200 cigarettes, 50 cigars or cigarillos, and 400 tobacco sticks or 400 grams of manufactured tobacco. Alcohol and tobacco must accompany you on your return.

An unlimited number of gifts valued up to C$60 each may be mailed to Canada duty-free. These do not count as part of your exemption. Label the package "Unsolicited Gift—Value under $60." Alcohol and tobacco are excluded.

For more information, including details of duties on items that exceed your duty-free limit, ask the Revenue Canada Customs and Taxation Department (2265 St. Laurent Blvd. S, Ottawa, Ontario, K1G 4K3, tel. 613/957–0275) for a copy of the free brochure "I Declare/Je Déclare."

Language

Spanish is the official language of Mexico, although Indian languages are spoken by approximately 20% of the population, many of whom speak no Spanish at all. Basic English is widely understood by most people employed in tourism, less so in the less developed areas. At the very least, shopkeepers will know the numbers for bargaining purposes.

As in most other foreign countries, knowing some words and phrases in the mother tongue has a way of opening doors. Mexicans are not scornful of visitors' mispronunciations and grammatical errors; on the contrary, they welcome even the most halting attempts to use their language.

The Spanish most Americans learn in high school is based on Castilian Spanish, which is as different from Latin American Spanish as British English or Continental French is from North

American English or French. Not only are there differences in pronunciation and grammar but also in vocabulary: Words or phrases that are harmless or everyday in one Spanish-speaking country can take on salacious or otherwise offensive meanings in another. Unless you are lucky enough to be briefed on these nuances by a native coach, the only way to learn is by trial and error.

Staying Healthy

Many travelers are eventually hit with an intestinal ailment known facetiously as Montezuma's Revenge or the Aztec Two-Step. Generally, it lasts only a day or two. A good antidiarrheal agent is paregoric, which dulls or eliminates abdominal cramps. You will need a doctor's prescription to get it in Mexico. The National Institute of Health recommends Pepto-Bismol and loperamide (Imodium) for mild cases of diarrhea. Lomotil is no longer recommended because it usually prolongs the infection. If you get sick, rest as much as possible, drink lots of fluids (such as tea without milk), and, in severe cases, rehydrate yourself with oral rehydration salts (ORS), widely available at Mexican pharmacies, added to purified water. The best defense against food and waterborne diseases is a smart diet. Stay away from unbottled or unboiled water, ice, raw food, unpasteurized milk, and milk products. Outdoor food stalls lacking refrigeration and proper sanitary facilities should also be avoided.

Caution is advised when venturing out in the Mexican sun. Sunbathers lulled by a slightly overcast sky or the sea breezes can be burned badly with as little as 20 minutes' exposure. Use strong sunscreens, and avoid the peak sun hours of noon to 2 PM.

Scuba divers take note: PADI recommends that you not scuba dive and fly within a 24-hour period.

Finding a Doctor The **International Association for Medical Assistance to Travellers** (IAMAT, 417 Center St., Lewiston, NY 14092, tel. 716/754–4883; 40 Regal Rd., Guelph, Ontario N1K 1B5; 57 Voirets, 1212 Grand-Lancy, Geneva, Switzerland) publishes a worldwide directory of English-speaking physicians whose qualifications meet IAMAT standards and who have agreed to treat members for a set fee. Membership is free.

Car Rentals

When considering this option, remember that Mexico is still a developing country. Acquiring a driver's license is sometimes more a question of paying someone off than of having tested skill, and the highway system is very uneven: in some regions, modern, well-paved super highways prevail; in others, particularly the mountains, potholes and dangerous, unrailed curves are the rule.

Many major car-rental companies are represented in Mexico, including **Avis** (tel. 800/331–1212, 800/879–2847 in Canada); **Budget** (tel. 800/527–0700); **Dollar** (tel. 800/800–4000); **Hertz** (tel. 800/654–3131, 800/263–0600 in Canada); and **National Interrent** (tel. 800/227–3876), known internationally as Tilden Interrent and Europcar Interrent. Mexico also has its own national and local firms (their rates are frequently less expensive). In cities, unlimited-mileage rates range from $34 per day for an economy car to $115 for a large car; weekly unlimited-mileage rates range from $306 to $477. This does not include tax, which in Mexico is 10% on car rentals.

Requirements Your own U.S., U.K., or Canadian driver's license is acceptable. Mexican rental agencies are more familiar with U.S. and Canadian licenses than with the international driver's licenses issued by the American Automobile Association, which must be obtained before you leave home. You will need to leave a deposit—the most acceptable being a blank, signed credit card voucher. Without a credit card, you will probably not be able to rent a car. Note that many car-rental agencies have minimum age requirements, ranging from 20 to 25.

When you drive in Mexico, it is necessary at all times to carry proof of Mexican auto liability insurance, which is usually provided by car-rental agencies and included in the cost of the rental. If you don't have proof of insurance and happen to injure someone—whether it's your fault or not—you stand the risk of being jailed.

Extra Charges Automatic transmissions and air-conditioning are not universally available; ask for them when you book if you want them, and check the cost before you commit yourself to the rental.

Arriving and Departing

By Plane

From the United States to Acapulco: **American** (tel. 800/433–7300) has nonstop flights from Dallas and connections from Chicago and New York through Dallas. **Continental** (tel. 800/528–1234) has nonstop service from Houston. **Delta's** (tel. 800/241–4141) nonstop service is from Los Angeles. **Mexicana** (tel. 800/531–7921) has nonstop service from Chicago and connecting service from New York, Miami, Los Angeles, San Antonio, San Francisco, and San Jose, California, all via Mexico City. **Aeromexico's** (tel. 800/237–6639) flight from New York to Acapulco stops in Mexico City. Other major carriers fly into Mexico City, where you can make a connection to Acapulco.

From New York via Dallas, flying time is 4½ hours; from Chicago, 4¼ hours; from Los Angeles, 3½ hours.

Between the Airport and City Center Private taxis are not permitted to carry passengers from the airport to town, so most people rely on **Transportes Terrestres,** a special airport taxi service. The bus system looks confusing, but there are dozens of helpful English-speaking staff to help you figure out which bus to take.

Look for the name of your hotel and the number of its zone on the overhead sign on the walkway in front of the terminal. Go to the desk for your zone and buy a ticket for an airport taxi that goes to your zone. The ride from the airport to the hotel zone on the trip costs about $6 per person for the *colectivo*, $36 for a private cab. The drivers are usually helpful and will often take you to hotels that aren't on their list. Tips are optional. The journey into town takes 20 to 30 minutes.

Smoking   Smoking is permitted aboard all Mexican airlines, but they do provide no-smoking sections. The International Civil Aviation Organization has set July 1, 1996, as the date to ban smoking aboard airlines worldwide, but the body has no power to enforce its decisions.

By Car

There are two absolutely essential things to remember about driving in Mexico. First and foremost is to carry Mexican auto insurance, which can be purchased near border crossings on either the U.S. or Mexican side. If you injure anyone in an accident, you could well be jailed—whether it was your fault or not—unless you have insurance. Guilty until proven innocent is part of the country's Code Napoléon.

The second item is that if you enter Mexico with a car, you must leave with it, the reason being that cars are much cheaper in the United States, and you are not allowed to sell your vehicle in Mexico. The fact that you drove in with a car is stamped on your tourist card, which you must give to immigration authorities at departure. If an emergency arises and you must fly home, you will have to deal with complicated customs procedures.

The trip to Acapulco from Mexico City on the old road takes about six hours. A new, privately built and run four-lane toll road connecting Mexico City with Acapulco is expensive (about $90 one-way) but well maintained, and it cuts driving time between the two cities from six hours to 3½ hours. Many people opt for going via Taxco, which can be reached from either road.

By Train, Bus, and Ship

By Train   There is no train service to Acapulco from any-
and Bus   where in the United States or Canada. Buses to Acapulco can be boarded on the U.S. side of the border, but the trip is not recommended; even the most experienced travelers find the journey exhausting and uncomfortable. Bus service from Mexico City to Acapulco, however, is excel-

lent. First-class buses are comfortable and in good condition, and the trip takes 5 hours. They leave every hour on the half-hour from the Tasqueña station. A first-class ticket costs about $20, one way. There is also deluxe service, called *Servicio Diamante*, with airplanelike reclining seats, refreshments, rest rooms, air-conditioning, movies, and hostess service. The deluxe buses leave four times a day, also from the Tasqueña station, and cost about $42. *Futura* service (regular reclining seats, air-conditioning, and a rest room) costs $27.

By Ship Many cruises include Acapulco as part of their itinerary. Most originate from Los Angeles. *See* Cruises, *below.*

Staying in Acapulco

Important Addresses and Phone Numbers

Tourist Information The Secretaría de Turismo (SECTUR) operates an extremely helpful and efficient 24-hour hot line in Mexico City with multilingual experts providing information about the entire country. You can call toll-free from the United States (tel. 800/482–9832) or from within Mexico (tel. 800/90–392).

Consulates **United States** (Club del Sol Hotel, tel. 74/85–72–07); **Canada** (Club del Sol Hotel, tel. 74/85–66–21).

Emergencies **Police,** tel. 74/85–08–62. The **Red Cross** can be reached at tel. 74/84–41–22 or 74/84–41–23. Two reliable hospitals are **Hospital Privado Magallanes,** Wilfrido Massiue 2, tel. 74/85–65–44, and **Hospital Centro Médico,** J. Arevalo 99, tel. 74/82–46–92.

Doctors and Dentists Your hotel and the Secretaría de Turismo can locate an English-speaking doctor. But English-speaking doctors don't come cheap—house calls are about $150. The U.S. consular representative has a list of dentists and suggests Dr. Guadalupe Carmona, Costera Miguel Alemán 220–101, tel. 74/85–71–76, or Dr. Arturo Carmona, Costera Miguel Alemán 220, Suite 110, tel. 74/85–72–86.

English-language Bookstores English-language books and periodicals can be found at Sanborns, a reputable American-style department-store chain, and at the newsstands in some of the larger hotels. Many small newsstands and the Super-Super carry the *Mexico City News*, an English-language daily newspaper that occasionally carries articles about Acapulco.

Travel Agencies **American Express,** at Costera Miguel Alemán 709, tel. 74/84–55–50, and **Viajes Wagon-Lits,** at Scenic Highway 5255 (Las Brisas Hotel), tel. 74/94–09–91.

Getting Around

Getting around in Acapulco is quite simple. You can walk to many places and the bus costs only 30¢. Taxis cost less than they do in the United States, so most tourists quickly become avid taxi takers.

By Bus The buses tourists use the most are those that go from Puerto Marqués to Caleta and stop at the fairly conspicuous metal bus stops along the way. If you want to go from the zócalo to the Costera, catch the bus that says "La Base" (the naval base near the Hyatt Regency). This bus detours through Old Acapulco and returns to the Costera just east of the Ritz Hotel. If you want to follow the Costera for the entire route, take the bus marked "Hornos." Buses to Pie de la Cuesta or Puerto Marqués say so on the front. The Puerto Marqués bus runs about every half hour and is always crowded. If you are headed anywhere along the Costera Miguel Alemán, it's best to go by the Aca Tur bus. For 60¢ you can ride in deluxe, air-conditioned buses that travel up and down the main drag from the Hyatt to the Caleta hotels every 10 minutes.

By Taxi How much you pay depends on what type of taxi you get. Hotel taxis are the most expensive. A price list that all drivers adhere to is posted in hotel lobbies. Fares in town are usually about $1.50 to $5; to go from downtown to the Princess Hotel or Caleta beach is about $10 to $15. Hotel taxis are by far the plushest and are kept in the best condition.

Cabs that cruise with their roof light off occasionally carry a price list but usually charge by zone. You need to reach an agreement with these drivers, but the fare should be less than it would be at a hotel. There is a minimum charge of $1.50. Some taxis that cruise have hotel or restaurant names stenciled on the side but are not affiliated with an establishment. Before you go anywhere by cab, find out what the price should be and agree with the driver on a price.

The cheapest taxis are the little Volkswagens. Officially there is a $1.50 minimum charge, but many cab drivers don't stick to it. A normal— i.e., Mexican-priced—fare is $1 to go from the zócalo to American Express, but lots of luck getting a taxi driver to accept that from a tourist. Rates are about 50% higher at night, and though tipping is not expected, Mexicans usually leave small change.

You can also hire a taxi by the hour or the day. Prices vary from about $20 an hour for a hotel taxi to $15 an hour for a street taxi. Never let a taxi driver decide where you should eat or shop, since many get kickbacks from some of the smaller stores and restaurants.

By Horse and Carriage Buggy rides up and down the Costera are available on weekends. Bargain before you get in— they cost about $20 a half hour.

By Car For day trips and local sightseeing, engaging a car and driver (who often acts as a guide) for a day can be a hassle-free, more economical way to travel than renting a car and driving yourself. Hotel desks will know which taxi companies to call, and you can negotiate a price with the driver.

Telephones

Thanks to the privatization of Teléfonos de México in 1991, Mexico's phone service, long exasperatingly inefficient, is gradually being overhauled. In the meantime, the variety of public phones that exists in the country can be confusing at best. You'll see traditional black, square phones with push buttons or dials; although they have a coin slot on top, you may make local calls on them for free. Then there are the new blue or ivory push-button phones with digital screens. Some of these have coin slots that accept only old peso coins; the large, 1,000-peso coins (worth about 33¢) allow for ample local conversations. Other new phones have both a coin slot and an unmarked slot; the latter are for LADATEL (Spanish acronym for "long-distance direct dialing") cards, handy magnetic-strip debit cards that can be purchased at tourist offices as well as at newsstands and stores with a LADATEL logo. They come in denominations of up to NP$50 (about $17) and can be used for both local and long-distance calls. Still other phones have two unmarked slots, one for a LADATEL card and the other for a credit card. These are primarily for Mexican bank cards, but some accept U.S. Visa or MasterCard, though *not* U.S. telephone credit cards.

To make a long-distance direct-dial call within Mexico, dial 91 + city area code + local number; for calls to the United States, dial 95 + city area code + local number. (Mexican area codes range from one to three digits—the larger the city, the fewer the digits.) To reach the local operator, dial 02. To reach an international operator, dial 09. The number for information is 04. To access AT&T's USA DIRECT service from the new push-button public phones, dial 01 or 95/800/462–4240; no coins or cards are required. The MCI access number is 95/800/674–7000. The only way to call a U.S. 800 number from Mexico is by using either AT&T or MCI (a charge will be billed to your credit card). Keep in mind that hotels add a hefty surcharge and tax on all long-distance calls placed through the hotel operator or the Mexico long-distance operator, as well as on direct-dial long-distance calls; there's also a surcharge for accessing AT&T or MCI from your hotel room. You're better off using the LADATEL phones found in many hotel lobbies.

The country code for Mexico is 52. Acapulco's area code is 74.

Mail

The Mexican postal system is notoriously slow and unreliable; *never* send, or expect to receive, packages, as they may be stolen (for emergencies, use a courier service or the new express-mail service, with insurance). There are post offices (*oficinas de correos*) even in the smallest villages, and numerous branches in the larger cities. Always use airmail for overseas correspondence; it will take anywhere from 10 days to two weeks or more, where surface mail might take three weeks to arrive. Service within Mexico can be equally slow. Postcard rates are NP$1.5 to the United States and NP$2.1 to Great Britain. Letters cost NP$2 to the United States and NP$2.8 to Great Britain.

To receive mail in Mexico, you can have it sent to your hotel or use *poste restante* at the post office. In the latter case, include the words "a/c Lista de Correos" (general delivery), followed by the city, state, postal code, and country. A list of names for whom mail has been received is posted and updated daily by the post office. American Express cardholders or traveler's check holders can have mail sent to them at the local American Express office. For a list of the offices worldwide, write for the *Traveler's Companion* from American Express (Box 678, Canal Street Station, New York, NY 10013), or pick one up at any American Express office.

Addresses

Many Mexican addresses have "s/n" for *sin número* (no number) after the street name. This is common in small towns where there are fewer buildings on a block. Similarly, many hotels give their address as "Km 30 a Querétaro," which indicates that the property is on the main highway 30 kilometers from Querétaro.

As in Europe, addresses in Mexico are written with the street name first, followed by the street number. The five-digit zip code (*código postal*) precedes, rather than follows, the name of the city. "Apdo." (*apartado*) means "post office box number."

Veteran travelers to Mexico invariably make one observation about asking directions in the country: Rather than say they do not know, Mexicans tend to offer guidance that may or may not be correct. This is not out of malice, but out of a desire to please. Therefore, patience is a virtue when tracking down an address.

Tipping

When tipping in Mexico, remember that the minimum wage is the equivalent of $6 a day and that the vast majority of workers in the tourist industry live barely above the poverty line. However, there are Mexicans who think in dollars and know, for example, that in the United States porters are tipped about $1 a bag; many of them expect the peso equivalent from foreigners (NP$3 at press time) but are happy to accept NP$1 from Mexicans. They will complain either verbally or with a facial expression if they feel they deserve more—you and your conscience must decide. Overtipping, however, is equally a problem. Following are some general guidelines, in pesos.

Porters and bellboys at airports and at moderate and inexpensive hotels: NP$2 per bag
Porters at expensive hotels: NP$4 per bag
Hotel room service: NP$3 (*Expensive*); NP$1 (*Moderate* and *Inexpensive*)
Maids: NP$2 per night (all hotels)
Waiters: 10%–15% of the bill, depending on service (make sure a 10%–15% service charge has not already been added to the bill, although this practice is not common in Mexico)
Taxi drivers: a 5%–10% tip is appreciated but not necessary.
Gas station attendants: 50 centavos
Parking attendants and theater ushers: NP$2–NP$3; some theaters have set rates

Opening and Closing Times

Banks are open weekdays 9 AM–1:30 PM. In some larger cities, a few banks also open weekdays 4–6 PM, Saturday 10 AM–1:30 PM and 4–6 PM, and Sunday 10 AM–1:30 PM; however, the extended hours are often for deposits only. Banks will give you cash advances in pesos (for a fee) if you have a major credit card. **Stores** are generally open weekdays and Saturday from 9 or 10 AM to 7 or 8 PM; in resort areas, they may also be open on Sunday. Business hours are 9 AM–7 PM, with a two-hour lunch break (siesta) from about 2 to 4 PM. **Govern-**

ment offices are usually open 8 AM–3 PM. All government offices, banks, and most private offices are closed on national holidays. **Museums, theaters, and most archaeological zones** close Monday, with few exceptions.

Credit Cards

The following credit card abbreviations are used throughout this guide: AE, American Express; DC, Diners Club; MC, MasterCard; V, Visa.

Cruises

Cruising the Mexican Riviera is perhaps the most relaxing and convenient way to tour this beautiful part of the world: You get all of the amenities of a luxury hotel and enough activities to guarantee fun. Cruising along the coast is an entirely different experience from staying on the mainland.

As a vacation, a cruise offers total peace of mind. All important decisions are made long before boarding the ship. The itinerary is set in advance, and the costs are known ahead of time and are all-inclusive, with no additional charge for meals, accommodations, entertainment, or recreational activities. (Only tips, shore excursions, bar tabs, and gambling losses are extra.) A cruise ship is a floating resort. For details beyond the basics, given below, see *Fodor's Cruises and Ports of Call 1995.*

When to Go

Loop cruises of 3, 4, 7, and sometimes 10 days usually depart from Los Angeles for the Mexican Riviera, calling at such ports as Acapulco, Puerto Vallarta, and Mazatlán. November through March is the cruising season—most ships reposition to Alaska for the summer. Still, it is possible to cruise here year-round, and prices are lowest from April through October.

June has the best weather, though it is remarkably good almost all year, with daytime temperatues averaging from 82°F to 90°F. During the June–October rainy season, very brief showers can be expected.

Choosing a Cabin

Write to the cruise line or ask your travel agent for a ship's plan. This elaborate layout, with cabins numbered, will show you all facilities available on all decks (usually, the higher the deck, the higher the prices). Outside cabins have portholes or picture windows that contribute to the romance of cruising, and, though usually sealed shut, may provide expansive sea views. Some windows overlook a public promenade, probably less desirable. Inside cabins are less expensive, but check the plan—you don't want to be over the galley, near the engine room, or next to the elevators. Those prone to motion sickness would do best in a cabin at midship, on one of the middle decks. The higher you go, the more motion you'll experience.

Tipping

Although some ships have no-tipping policies, tipping is a major expense on most Mexican Riviera ships. The ship's service personnel depend on tips for their livelihood, and you may feel pressure to help them out. It is customary to tip the cabin steward, the dining-room waiter, and the busboy; you may also tip the maître d', the wine steward, and the bartender for exceptional service. Most cruise lines distribute guidelines with suggested amounts the night before the voyage ends—which is when gratuities are normally given. Everyone wants a dollar, but not everyone expects one. It is wise to carry some pesos for those times when a dollar tip is too much. Don't tip less than NP$2.

Shore Excursions

Not surprisingly, some of the best excursions are those that take advantage of the area's wonderful beaches, where passengers indulge in parasailing, waterskiing, snorkeling, and windsurfing. Sunset sails and booze cruises are also popular.

Deep-sea fishing has long drawn sport-fishing fans hoping to land trophy-size marlin and sailfish, as well as tuna, wahoo, and bonito. Most ships sailing the Mexican Riviera offer half-day or full-day fishing at rates comparable to what it would cost to charter a boat on your own. It's therefore prudent to take the ship-organized excursions: The locals' relaxed sense of time is not shared by cruise-ship captains, who will—and do—leave without late passengers.

And be wary of land tours. A substantial percentage of the bus tours range from mediocre to indifferent. Too often, guides speak poor English, the vehicles are in poor repair, and the tour itself is of limited interest. Typically, a bus tour of the *ciudad* (city) will drive past the *malecón* (sea wall), stop briefly at the central cathedral on the *zócalo* (main town square)—and then, bypassing the few historic sites or authentic native markets, pull up at various hotels and time-share properties, where passengers are subjected to a sales pitch. Finally, passengers will be taken for an extended stop at a shopping area or crafts shop. While a few superb folkloric shows exist, most dance companies seen on bus tours are either young amateurs or jaded semiprofessionals who merely go through the motions.

Taxis are a worthwhile alternative to the bus tour, especially in Acapulco and Ixtapa/Zihuatanejo. Cabs are numerous and relatively cheap, and every driver accepts dollars. Taxis are not metered, however, nor are there fixed rates to specific destinations. Don't get in until you've negotiated an exact fare (including tip), and never pay the driver in advance. The cruise director usually knows the appropriate fare to various destinations, or how much it costs to hire a taxi by the hour. Not all taxi drivers are qualified to act as tour guides, however, and cabs almost never have air-conditioning.

Cruise Lines

Usually, the best deal on cruise bookings can be found by consulting a cruise-only travel agency. Contact the **National Association of Cruise Only Travel Agencies (NACOA)** (Box 7209. Freeport, NY 11520) for a listing of member firms in a particular state. Enclose a self-addressed stamped envelope. The **Cruise Lines International Association** (CLIA) publishes a useful pamphlet entitled "Cruising Answers to Your Questions"; to order a copy send a self-addressed business-size envelope with 52¢ postage to CLIA (500 5th Ave., Suite 1407, New York, NY 10110).

The following cruise lines stop in Acapulco.

Crystal Cruises (2121 Ave. of the Stars, Los Angeles, CA 90067, tel. 800/446–6645).
Cunard Line (555 5th Ave., New York, NY 10017, tel. 800/221–4770).
Holland America Line (300 Elliott Ave. W, Seattle, WA 98119, tel. 800/426–0327).
Princess Cruises (10100 Santa Monica Blvd., Los Angeles, CA 90067, tel. 310/553–1770).
Regency Cruises (260 Madison Ave., New York, NY 10016, tel. 212/972–4499).
Royal Caribbean Cruise Line (1050 Caribbean Way, Miami, FL 33132, tel. 800/327–6700).
Royal Cruise Line (1 Maritime Plaza, San Francisco, CA 94111, tel. 415/956–7200).
Silversea Cruises (110 E. Broward Blvd., Fort Lauderdale, FL 33301, tel. 305/522–4477 or 800/722–6655).

2 Portraits of Acapulco

Host to the World

by Erica
Meltzer

*A writer and
translator
whose
specialty is
Mexico,
Erica has
been a
frequent
visitor there
since 1967,
and has lived
in Mexico
City.*

The story of Acapulco begins with a Romeo-and-Juliet-like myth of the Yope Indians, who had been driven to Acapulco from the north by the Nahuas, forerunners of the Aztecs. Acatl (his name means "reed"), firstborn son of the tribal chief, heard a voice telling him that in order to perpetuate his race, he should seek the love of Quiahuitl ("rain"), daughter of an enemy chieftain. But after the two fell in love, her father refused to allow the marriage. Grief-stricken, Acatl returned to his home in the foothills of the Sierra Madre above the Bay of Acapulco, intent on being devoured by the animals. But Acatl missed the sweet warbling of the *zenzontle* bird and returned to the bay to lie beneath the mesquite tree, where he wept so hard that his body dissolved into a puddle of mud, which spread across the coastal plain. From the mud sprang little reeds, yellowish green tinged with red: These were the sons of Acatl, bearing the colors of the mesquite and the zenzontle. Quiahuitl, in turn, was transformed into an immense cloud and floated toward the bay where, finding her lost love, she dissolved in tears. The teardrops fell on the reeds, and Quiahuitl was united forever with Acatl. This is said to be the origin of the name Acapulco, which means "in the place where the reeds were destroyed." The legend holds that whenever the bay is threatened by clouds, Quiahuitl, remembering her love, is returning.

Acapulco has been inhabited since at least 3000 BC; the oldest Nahua artifacts in the region date from 2,000 years ago. These artifacts—clay heads, known as the "Pretty Ladies of Acapulco"—were discovered in the lost city of La Sabana, in the hills outside

Acapulco. Because of earthquakes, the region contains few other archaeological remains.

From 1486 to 1502, after centuries under Toltec rule, Acapulco became part of the Aztec empire. It was then taken over by the Tarascans, another Indian tribe, along with the rest of the province of Zacatula. It was such power struggles among the Indians that eventually led to Acapulco's conquest by the Spaniards under Hernán Cortés. Montezuma II, the Aztec emperor, told Cortés that more gold came from Zacatula than from anywhere else so that Cortés would conquer Montezuma's rivals, the Tarascans, and leave his realm alone.

Acapulco was discovered by Francisco Chico on December 13, 1521, and has been a magnet for seekers of wealth ever since. Chico had been sent by Cortés to find sites for ports, since Cortés was obsessed with locating a route to the Spice Islands. Acapulco has a great natural harbor, twice as deep as either San Francisco or New York, and so was a perfect choice. In accordance with a custom of Spanish explorers, Chico named the bay after the saint whose feast day coincided with the day of his landing: Santa Lucía. Cortés then built a mule path from Mexico City to Acapulco—his Spanish overlords forbade the use of Indians to transport cargo —and used the settlement to build ships for his explorations of the South Pacific. In 1532, the town officially became a domain of the Spanish crown, known as the *Ciudad de los Reyes*, or City of the Kings. Cortés went frequently to Acapulco, staying at Puerto Marqués Bay, which was named for him (Cortés was the marquis, or Marqués, of the Valley of Oaxaca).

By 1579, Acapulco was booming, and King Philip II decreed it the only official port for trade between America and Asia—primarily the Philippines, which had been discovered by Spaniards sailing from Acapulco. (In the Spanish spoken in the Philippines, *acapulco* is the name of a plant, the *Cassia alata*, introduced to the Philippines by traders from Mexico.) For centuries afterward, the port played a crucial role in the history of the New World: In 1537, Cortés sent ships to Francisco Pizarro to help his conquest of Peru, and two years later he launched an expedition to discover the Seven Cities of Cíbola. Ships from Acapulco explored Cape Mendocino, California, in 1602.

But it was the Manila galleons—the *naos de China*—that brought Acapulco its early fame. The first vessel, the *San Pablo*, sailed in 1565, and for the next 250 years the Spanish crown maintained a stranglehold on trade with the Orient. The naos carried the richest cargo of their day: silks, porcelain, cottons, rugs, jade, ivory, incense, spices, and slaves. When goods from the East reached Acapulco, they were then carried overland—a 20-day journey along the six-foot-wide Road to Asia trail—to Veracruz on the Gulf of Mexico, where other ships then bore the cargo to Europe. On their return voyages to the East, the galleons transported silver from Mexico and Peru. The Spaniards limited the traffic to one arrival a year, usually at Christmas, and this event was heralded by the great Acapulco Fair of the Americas. Traders and merchants came from all over New Spain to buy the goods, and the malaria-ridden village, normally home to 4,000 people (mostly blacks and mulattoes), was suddenly host to 12,000. Thus, from its early days, Acapulco became well versed in the arts of hospitality. Because accommodations were insufficient to lodge the flood of visitors, locals developed a lucrative business by renting out houses, patios, corrals, and even doorways. They made fortunes as entertainers, quack doctors, porters, food vendors, and water carriers. Visitors amused themselves with bullfights, cockfights, and horse races. So much Peruvian gold and silver changed hands that the mules were literally laden with coins, and the Spanish crown was obliged to remint the precious metals and exploit the Mexican silver mines.

All this wealth had several unfortunate consequences for Acapulco and New Spain. One was that the monopolies enjoyed by the guilds of Acapulco and Veracruz kept prices high and the demand for locally produced goods low. Eventually the Spaniards allowed two overland journeys a year and established other ports to relieve the trade bottleneck.

The other outcome was the arrival of pirates. Until Sir Francis Drake's *Golden Hind* first sailed into Acapulco Bay in his exploration of the Pacific, the riches of the Manila galleons were a Spanish secret. Drake, whose ship was shot at by panicking Spaniards, boarded their ship, stole the map to Manila, and a few days later intercepted one of the galleons. Drake informed Queen Elizabeth of his windfall, and from that day on, Acapulco was under constant siege by the likes of British pirates Thomas Cavendish, Henry Morgan, and William Dampier. (Treasure is still said to be buried off Roqueta Island.) The galleon crews arriving from Manila, exhausted from their journey and from malnutrition (food generally rotted during the long sea voyages), were never a match for the corsairs (English pirates), well fed from the excellent fishing in the Gulf of California. The first fort, the Castillo de San Diego, was built in 1616, and even it could not stave off the Dutch Prince of Nassau, who pillaged the city in 1624.

An earthquake destroyed the fort in 1776; its replacement, the Fuerte de San Diego, dates from 1783. In 1799, King Carlos IV declared Acapulco an official city, but shortly thereafter, its decline set in. With the independence movement in 1810, the fair was suspended; the arriving nao found the beaches deserted, and the captain was told to take his ship to San Blas. That same year insurgent leader José Maria Morelos attacked Acapulco, and a long and bloody siege ensued. The Acapulqueños, who were not particularly enthused by the prospect of losing the source of their livelihood, preferred continued allegiance with the Spanish empire to the dubitable gains of independence. Acapulco, an important source of revenue for Spain, was a natural target for the rebels, and Morelos burned it in 1814 to destroy its value.

Despite a devastating cholera outbreak in 1850, Acapulco enjoyed a brief revival in the 1850s, an outcome of the California gold rush. Ships stopped in Acapulco on their way to the Isthmus of Panama and returned to San Francisco carrying Mexican textiles. (Coincidentally, the great-grandson of "49er" John Sutter, Ricardo Morlet Sutter, was Acapulco's municipal president in the 1960s.) And in 1855 Benito Juárez, widely considered the father of modern Mexico, was sent to Acapulco to help bring down the dictator Antonio Santa Anna. A few years later, the city was bombarded by a French squadron during Juárez's fight against Emperor Maximilian, who had recognized Acapulco's strategic importance.

Acapulco resumed its fitful slumber through most of the 19th and early 20th centuries. An earthquake nearly razed the city in 1909; two years later it was invaded by some rebellious *lobos*—Afro-Indians from the neighboring Costa Chica region descended from escaped slaves—who threw off the yoke of a tyrant,

Johann Schmidt, during the early years of the Mexican Revolution. Modern Acapulco dates from the 1920s, when wealthy Mexicans—and adventurous gringos—began frequenting the somnolent village. With the opening of the first highway along Cortés's mule trail in 1928 and initial air service from the capital in 1929, Acapulco began to attract the Hollywood crowd and international statesmen. President Lázaro Cárdenas (1934–40) started public works; the first telephone service began in 1936.

Ironically, it was Cárdenas's nationalism that modernized Mexico's hotel industry, thereby paving the way for the early foreign hotel entrepreneurs who would later dominate that sector of the economy. Cárdenas prohibited foreigners both from owning property within 50 kilometers of the Mexican coastline and from buying hotels. Foreigners circumvented the law either by becoming Mexican citizens or by setting up dummy corporations.

Thus it was a Texan, Albert B. Pullen, who first formed a company in the 1930s to develop the beautiful Peninsula de las Playas—now known as Old Acapulco—where many of Acapulco's first hotels rose. Pullen became a millionaire in the process, and a real estate boom soon followed. J. Paul Getty was alleged to have purchased 900 acres of land at 3 cents an acre, some of which he used to build the Pierre Marqués ("Pierre" after his New York hotel of that name, "Marqués" after Cortés). In 1933, Carlos Barnard erected his first bungalows at El Mirador, atop the cliffs at La Quebrada, and other hotels followed suit.

But despite the growing tourist traffic, Acapulco still had the look, and appeal, of a humble town. Writers flocked to it: the reclusive B. Traven, author of *Treasure of the Sierra*

Madre, ran a restaurant there from 1929 to 1947. Malcolm Lowry (*Under the Volcano*) first saw Mexico from his Acapulco-bound ship on November 2, 1936; that four-month sojourn was spent sampling the charms of tequila, pulque, mezcal, and Mexican beer. The playwright Sherwood Anderson visited Acapulco in 1938, and Tennessee Williams spent the summer of 1940 there. (Acapulco is, in fact, the setting for *The Night of the Iguana,* his celebrated play that John Huston later filmed in Puerto Vallarta.) That same year, Jane and Paul Bowles, the bohemian writer-couple, rented a house there, complete with avocado and lemon trees, a hammock, and their own tropical menagerie. At that time Acapulco boasted dirt roads, a wooden pier, no electricity, and a lot of mosquitoes.

Well-heeled foreigners first became interested in Acapulco during World War II, when most other pleasure spots were off-limits. In 1947, a two-lane highway improved accessibility, cutting travel time from Mexico City to a day and a half. By then there were 28,000 residents, compared to just 3,000 in 1931.

It was President Miguel Alemán Valdés (1946–52) who is credited with turning Acapulco into a tourist destination. Alemán ordered roads paved, streets laid out, water piped in, and public buildings erected. Even after his presidency, when he directed the newly formed National Tourism Council, Alemán was instrumental in the town's development. He was responsible for the new four-lane super-highway, which in 1955 made it possible to reach Acapulco from Mexico City in just six hours.

The jet-setters' invasion of Acapulco reached its peak in the 1940s and '50s. While many of them owned homes there, they still liked to congregate primarily at two hotels. Las

Brisas was built in 1954 as a small cottage col-
ony, Bermuda-style, by Juan March, on the
former site of the fortress. The other water-
ing hole was the Villa Vera Racquet Club.
Originally a private residence for an Omaha
businessman, it was later managed by Ernest
Henri ("Teddy") Stauffer, a Swiss swing
bandleader who had fled the Nazis and set-
tled in Acapulco, where he became affection-
ately known as "Mr. Acapulco." Stauffer also
put up Acapulco's first discotheque, Tequila
A Go-Go, and took over the popular La Perla
restaurant at La Quebrada, home to the cliff
divers. The Villa Vera boasted one of
Acapulco's many innovations, the first swim-
up bar, and its first tennis club. (Another
Acapulco first was parasailing.)

L ana Turner used to frequent the Villa
Vera's piano bar. Elizabeth Taylor mar-
ried Mike Todd there, with Debbie Reynolds
and Eddie Fisher as witnesses. JFK honey-
mooned in Acapulco, as did Brigitte Bardot
and, many years later, Henry Kissinger. Yu-
goslav President Tito stayed there for 38
days, in one of 76 private homes owned by
Las Brisas. President Eisenhower's visit in
1959 brought Acapulco even more publicity,
as did an international film festival that de-
buted that year. Acapulco's guest list filled
the society pages and gossip columns of
America and Europe: Frank Sinatra, Johnny
Weissmuller, New York Mayor Robert Wag-
ner, Harry Belafonte, Douglas Fairbanks,
Jr., Judy Garland, Sir Anthony Eden, John
Wayne, Gina Lollobrigida, Gary Cooper,
Edgar Bronfman, Jimmy Stewart, the
Guinness family, Richard Widmark, Baron
de Rothschild. . . .

By the late 1950s and early '60s, Acapulco,
which had also acquired the sobriquet "Nirvana by the Sea," was being called "Miami on
the Pacific." It had long since ceased to be the
exclusive haven for the rich and famous: Ho-

tel construction had mushroomed, and the city's infrastructure could not keep pace with the growing resident population, then 100,000. La Laja, a seedy cluster of tenements outside town lacking sewers, drinking water, and electricity, swelled with 8,000 minimum-wage hotel workers known as *paracaidistas* (parachutists), or squatters. The government tried discreetly to squelch the city's social problems by selling the land at La Laja to the squatters, but also feared that move would encourage even more migration and aggravate unemployment. Hundreds of locals—mostly Indians from the surrounding region—were reduced to roaming the beaches, peddling kitschy folk art, tie-dyed beachwear, suntan oil, and soda.

By the mid-1960s, the government was eyeing the Port of Acapulco with renewed interest as a way to balance the economy and offset the seasonality of tourism. Acapulco was again trading, primarily with the Orient, and in 1963 some 180 freighters arrived, laden with Japanese appliances and automobiles. Each year, 60,000 tons of copra—dried coconut meat, used for making soap and margarine—left port; the copra industry was second to tourism in the region. The government wanted to capitalize on Acapulco's revived trade status by building a new port and opening a railroad to convey all the imports and locally produced copra, rubber, and wood pulp to Mexico City. But the projects never got off the ground.

So tourism—which generated $50 million a year in direct spending—remained the key to Acapulco. With the advent of international jet travel in 1964, and the start-up of nonstop service from the United States in 1966, Acapulco's ascendancy became even more spectacular. The once lowly airport was dressed up in marble, and countless foreigners arrived to set up fashion boutiques and restaurants and indulge in the lucrative trade of marijuana and cocaine. Media stories continued to appear with great regularity, focusing largely on Merle Oberon Pagliai, the queen of Acapulco society, who spent six months a year in Acapulco in her Moorish-style villa, El Ghalal. Needless to say, that abode was as lavish as the nightly parties thrown about town by her fellow travelers, where socks were prohibited and themed events varied from disco nights (accompanied by the sounds of the Beach Boys) to costume frolics (all invitees dressed as Charles Addams's characters). *Coco locos*—a mouthful of coconut juice with a generous serving of rum, gin, or tequila, inevitably presented in a coconut shell—were all the rage.

But Acapulco's clients in the '60s—and today still—were not only the Beautiful People. The majority were actually Mexicans, to whom Acapulco was the equivalent of Atlantic City. In addition, there were vacationing college students—frequently indulging in midnight surf-dancing—seamen, and middle-class Americans who felt comfortable with the American-brand fast-food outlets lining the Costera Alemán, a south-of-the-border Coney Island.

Commercialization and unbridled growth took their toll on Acapulco in the 1970s. Belatedly, the government planned a $14 million project to pipe the city's sewage out to sea; prior to that the sewage had simply been carried in an open canal, and the hotels had installed their own services. Having reached the mature stage of its development, Acapulco found its glamour and popularity waning. That may have been a godsend for its 300,000 residents, crowded to the breaking point, as rural unrest in the surrounding countryside led increasingly to outbursts of violence. In the early 1970s, guerrillas assassinated Acapulco's police chief, kidnapped the state senator, and occasionally took hostages in Acapulco itself before most of the group was killed in gun battles.

As Acapulco waned, Mexico began looking elsewhere to practice its magic. In Ixtapa, Cancún, Los Cabos, and now Huatulco, the government is attempting to avoid the mistakes it made in Acapulco through careful planning, while duplicating its formula of sea, sand, and sex. Several of those destinations now siphon off the tourism business. Whereas in the 1960s foreigners represented 45% of Acapulco's tourist revenue, by the mid-1980s that figure had slipped to 32%.

But Acapulqueños, who for centuries have derived their livelihood from commerce with foreigners, are intent on keeping their city afloat. In 1988, the public and private sectors banded together to refurbish the area known as Traditional (or Old) Acapulco, centered on Caleta Beach and the Zócalo. Hotels are being spruced up, street vendors are being paid to relocate to public markets, and the streets are undergoing a face-lift. And although one-third of Acapulco's one million residents still live in slums, that fact seldom intrudes on the tourist's conscience. In terms of sheer size, Acapulco is still the biggest of Mexico's tourist destinations. To many, it continues to epitomize the glamour and vitality for which it has long been celebrated. And though it will go through more permutations, Acapulco holds a secure place in Mexico's future.

The Cliff Dive

by Craig Vetter

Chicago is home for freelance writer Craig Vetter.

Just before the divers at La Quebrada in Acapulco take the long fall from the cliff into the surf, they kneel at a little shrine to Our Lady of Guadalupe and say their prayers. It's not hard to imagine what they ask her—I used to know the prayers they know—probably something like, "Remember, O most gracious Virgin, that never was it known that anyone who fled to thy protection, implored thy help or sought thy intercession was left unaided. Inspired by this confidence, I fly to thee, O Virgin of Virgins, my Mother. To thee I come, before thee I stand, sinful and sorrowful. O Mother of the word incarnate, despise not my petitions but in thy mercy hear and answer me: Let the water be deep enough, let the current be gentle, save me from garbage on the water, from the rocks, from blindness, from death, and may the *turistas* drop at least ten pesos apiece into the hat before they haul their fat white bodies back onto the buses."

I watched them dive half a dozen times one day. I sat on the terrace of the Mirador Hotel that overlooks the cliff with tequila and beer in front of me, telling myself I was trying to decide whether or not I would do this thing. I knew that the power of prayer wouldn't get me into the air off that rock. I've dived from heights before, but never that high, never out over rocks like those, never into a slash of water as narrow as that. Still, the only reason I was down there in the good tropical sun was to dive or to come up with an eloquent string of reasons why I hadn't. As it was, every time

a Mexican dived, I was adding a because to
my list of why nots.

One of them would walk out onto the rock
and look down at the surf 130 feet below
him. Then he'd kneel at the shrine, cross him-
self and pray. When he got up, he'd wander
out of sight for a moment behind the little
statue of Mary, then come back and stand for
another five minutes on the edge while the
tourists crowded the railings of the hotel terrace and filled the vantage points on the
rocks below. Then he'd put both arms out
straight in front of him, drop them to his
sides, cock his legs, roll forward, and then
spring with what looked like all his strength
into a perfect flying arch. Foam boils up
where the divers go in and the sound when
they hit the water is like an old cannon going
off. Then, a few seconds later, he'd be up,
waving one arm and treading water against
the white surge that was trying to slap him
up onto the rocks.

After a couple of divers and a couple of
tequilas, I was telling myself I could live
through it. I'd probably get hurt real bad,
but it wouldn't kill me. I could get out past
those rocks, all right, then it would just be a
matter of going into the water as straight and
skinny and strong as I could. I figured the
worst I could get would be a broken back. Or
else . . . or else I could sit right there on that
terrace, have another shot of Cuervo, maybe
six, lay back on my laurels and review the
risks already taken. The worst I could get
would be a hangover.

One of the divers came around to collect 50
cents. I gave him a dollar and when he said
that was too much, I told him no, it wasn't.
His name was Fidel and he had a broad face
and a paunch that hung out over his tight red
trunks. He looked about 40 years old. I asked
him what kind of injuries the *clavadistas* got

when they didn't hit the water right. Broken bones, he told me, when the arms sometimes collapse into the head on impact. And the eyes, he said, if you break the water eyes first instead of with the top of your head, you go blind. But they have an association, he said, and the 26 divers in it have a fund, so that if one of them is hurt or killed, his family is taken care of. I didn't ask him if there was a fund for half-wit gringos with a history of foolish moments and a little too much sauce in them. There are no funds for people like that, people like me. Just simple services when the time comes.

Fidel moved off through the crowd, looking for more peso notes, and pretty much left me thinking there was no way in hell I was going to make that dive. The idea that I'd probably survive the plunge didn't mean nearly as much after he told me about the arms snapping over the head on entry. Somehow, I could *hear* that one. Even from 40 or 45 feet, which is the highest I've ever dived, you hit the water hard enough to make a moron out of yourself if you do it wrong. It *hurts* even when you do it right.

Finally, that afternoon, I figured out exactly what that cliff was to me. It wasn't a test of guts, or coordination, or strength, or Zen oneness with this imaginary existence. It was an intelligence test, the most fundamental kind of intelligence test: If you're intelligent, you don't *take* the test. Still, to sit there and think it through was one thing. I knew I had to let the animal make the final decision; take the meat up there onto that rock and let it look down the throat of this thing, let it *feel* the edge. There'd be no more maybes after that.

You actually have to climb down the rocks from the hotel to the spot from which they dive. On my way, I kept waiting for someone

to stop me, tell me it was divers only out
there, but no one did and there were no warn-
ing signs. I jumped a low stone wall and crept
down some rock steps overhung with trees
that made it feel like a tunnel out the end of
which I could see the backside of the little
shrine. It was cement, painted silver, and behind it, stacked like cordwood—as if to say
that even among religious people liquor takes
up where prayer leaves off—were two dozen
empty tequila bottles. Two steps beyond that
and I was out from under the green overhead
and on the small flat pad from which they do
it, and the scene opened before me: to my
left, the hotel. I could see people tapping
each other and pointing at me, as if to say,
"Here goes another one, Edith." To my right,
the flat blue Pacific stretched out to a sharp
tropical horizon, and then turned into sky. I
stepped up and hung my toes over the edge,
and then looked down at the rocks below me,
then at the rocks on the other side, then at
the skinny finger of water between them, ris-
ing and falling, foaming in and out. There
were Styrofoam cups on the tide, pieces of
cardboard and other trash I couldn't make
out. I remembered my mother, who was a
champion swimmer in the '30s, telling me
about a woman high diver who'd gone off a
100-foot tower in Atlantic City and hit an or-
ange peel on the water. She lived, but the im-
age of their hauling her limp from the water
has stayed with me, and it was never more
vivid than at that moment at La Quebrada.
Looking down from that cliff, your perspective is so hopelessly distorted it seems that,
to miss the rocks on your side of the channel,
you'd have to throw yourself onto the rocks on
the other side. I tried to imagine myself
through it. Get steady, feet together, arms
down, roll, push, arch . . . but I couldn't take
the fantasy any further than that. "No," I
said out loud. "Just turn around and say
goodbye to the Lady, Craig."

A couple of hours later, the defeat of the thing didn't seem very profound at all. If I'd kept drinking tequila, I just might have gone screaming off that cliff. Tequila, after all, talks to the animal in you and *he* thinks he can do anything when he's drunk.

After all, you gotta stop somewhere.

3 Exploring Acapulco

Acapulco is a city that is easily understood, easily explored. During the day the focus for most visitors is the beach and the myriad activities that happen on and off it—sunbathing, swimming, waterskiing, parasailing, snorkeling, deep-sea fishing, and so on. At night the attention shifts to the restaurants and discos. The Costera Miguel Alemán, the wide boulevard that hugs Acapulco Bay from the Scenic Highway to Caleta Beach (a little less than 8 kilometers, or 5 miles), is central to both day and night diversions. All the major beaches, big hotels—minus the more exclusive East Bay properties, such as Las Brisas, Sheraton, Camino Real, Pierre Marqués, and the Princess—and shopping malls are off the Costera. Hence most of the shopping, dining, and clubbing takes place within a few blocks of the Costera, and many an address is listed only as "Costera Miguel Alemán." Because street addresses are not often used and streets have no logical pattern, directions are usually given from a major landmark, such as CiCi or the zócalo.

Old Acapulco, the colonial part of town, is where the Mexicans go to run their errands: mail letters at the post office, buy supplies at the Mercado Municipal, and have clothes made or repaired at the tailor. Here is where you'll find the zócalo, the church, and Fort San Diego. Just up the hill from Old Acapulco is La Quebrada, where, five times a day, the cliff divers plunge into the surf 130 feet below.

The peninsula just south of Old Acapulco contains remnants of the first version of Acapulco. This primarily residential area has been prey to dilapidation and abandonment of late, and the efforts made to revitalize it—such as reopening the Caleta Hotel and opening the aquarium on Caleta Beach and the zoo on Roqueta Island—haven't met with much success. The Plaza de Toros, where bullfights are held on Sundays from Christmas to Easter, is in the center of the peninsula.

If you arrived by plane, you've had a royal introduction to Acapulco Bay. As you drive from the airport, via the Scenic Highway, the first thing you see on your left is the golf course for the

Acapulco Princess. Just over the hill is your first glimpse of the entire bay, and it is truly gorgeous, day or night.

Numbers in the margin correspond to points of interest on the Acapulco map.

❶ **La Base,** the Mexican naval base next to Plaza Icacos, anchors the eastern terminus of the Costera. There are no tours.

❷ The **Centro Cultural Guerrerense** is on the beach side of the Costera, just past the Hyatt Regency. It has a small archaeological museum and the Zochipala art gallery with changing exhibits. *Admission free. Open weekdays 9–1 and 5–8.*

❸ CiCi (short for Centro Internacional para Convivencia Infantil), on the Costera, is a water-oriented theme park for children. There are dolphin and seal shows, a freshwater pool with wave-making apparatus, water slide, mini-aquarium, and other attractions. *Admission: $10 adults, $8.50 children. Open daily 10–6.*

❹ About a half mile past CiCi, on the right side of the Costera, is **Centro Internacional** (the Convention Center), not really of interest unless you are attending a conference there. There is a **Mexican Fiesta** nightly at 8:15. There are three options: A buffet dinner (which begins at 7:30), open bar, and show costs $42; the show and open bar, without dinner, is $23; entrance to the show alone is $16.

❺ Continue along through the heart of the Costera until you reach **Papagayo Park,** one of the top municipal parks in the country. Named for the hotel that formerly occupied the grounds, Papagayo sits on 52 acres of prime real estate on the Costera, just after the underpass at the end of this strip. Youngsters enjoy the life-size model of a Spanish galleon like the ones that once sailed into Acapulco when it was Mexico's capital of trade with the Orient. There is an aviary, a roller-skating rink, a racetrack with mite-size racecars, a replica of the space shuttle *Columbia*, bumper boats in a lagoon, and other rides. *Small fee to enter; rides cost $1–$3.50. Open daily 10–6.*

❻ The sprawling **Mercado Municipal,** a few blocks west of the Costera, is Acapulco at its most authentic. Locals come to purchase their everyday needs, from fresh vegetables and candles to plastic buckets and love potions. Go between 10 AM and 1 PM and ask to be dropped off near the *flores* (flower stand) closest to the souvenir and crafts section. If you've driven to the mercado, locals may volunteer to watch your car; be sure to lock your trunk and tip about 35¢.

The stalls within the mercado are densely packed together but luckily are awning-covered, so things stay quite cool despite the lack of air-conditioning. From the flower stall, as you face the ceramic stand, turn right and head into the market. There are hundreds of souvenirs to choose from: woven blankets, puppets, colorful wooden toys and plates, leather goods, baskets, hammocks, and handmade wooden furniture including child-size chairs. There is even a stand offering charms, amulets and talismans, bones, herbs, fish eyes, sharks' teeth, lotions, candles, and soaps said to help one find or keep a mate, increase virility or fertility, bring peace to the home, or ward off the evil eye. You can also find some kitschy gems: Acapulco ashtrays and boxes covered with tiny shells or enormous framed pictures of the Virgin of Guadalupe. There are also silver jewelry vendors, but unless you really have a good eye for quality, it's best to buy silver only from a reputable dealer (*see* Chapter 4, Shopping).

❼ Built in the 18th century to protect the city from pirates, **El Fuerte de San Diego** is on the hill overlooking the harbor next to the army barracks in Old Acapulco. (The original fort, destroyed in an earthquake, was built in 1616.) The fort now houses the **Museo Histórico de Acapulco,** under the auspices of Mexico City's prestigious Museum of Anthropology. The exhibits portray the city from prehistoric times through Mexico's independence from Spain in 1821. Especially noteworthy are the displays touching on the Christian missionaries sent from Mexico to the Far East and the cultural interchange that resulted. *Tel. 74/82–38–28. Admission: $4.20. Open Tues.–Sun. 10:30–5.*

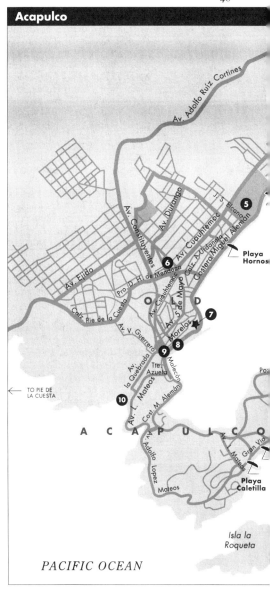

Acapulco

Av. Adolfo Ruiz Cortines

Av. Constituyentes

Av. Durango

J. J. S. Elcano

5

Av. Cuauhtémoc

Cuz. B. Urdaneta

Costera Miguel Alemán

Playa Hornos

Av. Ejido

Pro. D. H. de Mendoza

6

O L D

Av. Cuauhtémoc

Av. 5 de Mayo

Morelos

7

Calz. Pie de la Cuesta

Av. V. Guerrero

9

8

Malecón

Tte. Azueta

Av. la Quebrada

← TO PIE DE LA CUESTA

Av. L. Mateos

10

Cost. M. Alemán

A C A P U L C O

Av. Adolfo López

Mateos

Mateos

Poz

Gran Vía

Playa Caletilla

Isla la Roqueta

PACIFIC OCEAN

Av. Rancho
Acapulco

Paseo del Farallon

Cuauhtemoc

Av. M...tel

Diana
Glorieta

Costera Miguel Alemán

Playa
Condesa

Playa
Hornitos

Golf
Course

Lobo Solitario

Av. Almirante de Hidaca Nelson

Av. Almirante de Magallanes

Costera Miguel Alemán

Costera Miguel Alemán

Playa
Icacos

4

3

2

1

Punta
Guitarrón

*Bahía de
Acapulco*

Carretera

Escénica

E A S T

B A Y

TO AIRPORT →

del Rey
v

opical

Playa
Caleta

Punta Bruja

*Bahía de
Puerto
Marqués*

Playa
Roqueta

TO PUNTA DIAMANTE →
AND BARRA VIEJA

N

| 0 | 880 yards |
| 0 | 800 meters |

❽ Acapulco is still a lively commercial port and fishing center. If you stroll along the **waterfront,** you'll see all these activities at the commercial docks. The cruise ships dock here, and at night Mexican parents bring their children to play on the small treelined promenade. Farther west, by the zócalo, are the docks for the sightseeing yachts and smaller fishing boats. It's a good spot to join the Mexicans in people-watching.

❾ The **zócalo** is the center of Old Acapulco, a shaded plaza in front of **Nuestra Señora de la Soledad,** the town's modern but unusual—stark-white exterior with bulb-shaped blue and yellow spires—church. Overgrown with dense trees, the zócalo is the hub of downtown. All day it's filled with vendors, shoeshine men, and people lining up to use the pay phones. After siesta, they drift here to meet and greet. On Sunday evenings there's music in the bandstand. There are several cafés and newsagents selling the English-language *Mexico City News,* so tourists lodging in the area linger here, too. Just off the zócalo, Sanborns attracts locals and tourists alike; many linger for hours over the newspaper and a cup of coffee. Around the zócalo are several souvenir shops, and on the side streets you can get hefty, fruity milk shakes for about $1. The flea market, inexpensive tailor shops, and Woolworth's (*see* Chapter 4, Shopping) are nearby.

Time Out | The café at 45 Cinco de Mayo, below the German restaurant, serves *churros* every afternoon beginning at 4. This Spanish treat of fried dough dusted with sugar and dipped in hot chocolate is popular at *merienda*, which means "snack."

❿ A 10-minute walk up the hill from the zócalo brings you to **La Quebrada.** This is home to the famous Mirador Hotel. In the 1940s this was the center of action for tourists, and it retains an atmosphere reminiscent of its glory days. Most visitors eventually make the trip here because this is where the famous cliff divers jump from a height of 130 feet daily at 1 PM and evenings at 7:30, 8:30, 9:30, and 10:30. The dives are thrilling, so be sure to arrive early. Before they dive, the brave divers say a prayer at a small shrine near

the jumping-off point. Sometimes they dive in
pairs; often they carry torches.

What to See and Do with Children

CiCi and **Papagayo Park** (*see above*). Children
might also like to see the aquarium on Caleta
beach, where there are also swimming pools, a
toboggan, scuba diving, and (for rent) Jet Skis,
inner tubes, bananas (inflatable rubber tubes
pulled along the beach by motorboats), and kay-
aks—not to mention clean rest rooms. From
here you can take the launch to Roqueta Island
for a visit to the small zoo, or a glass-bottomed
boat to La Quebrada and Puerto Marqués.
*Aquarium admission: $7 adults, $5 children.
Ferry service to Roqueta Island, including zoo
admission: $4. Glass-bottomed boat: $7.*
Palao's. This restaurant on Roqueta Island has a
sandy cove for swimming, a pony, and a cage of
monkeys that entertain the youngsters. Children enjoy the motorboat ride out to the island.
Other good restaurants for children are **Beto's,
Mimi's Chili Saloon,** and **Carlos 'n' Charlie's** (*see*
Chapter 6, Dining).

4   Shopping

There is quite a lot of shopping to do in Acapulco, and the abundance of air-conditioned shopping malls and boutiques makes picking up gifts and souvenirs all the more pleasurable. Except for the markets, most places close for siesta. The typical hours of business are 10–1 and then 4–7, though these hours vary slightly. Most shops close on Sunday.

Though the peso has been stabilized, the exchange rate still gives travelers to Acapulco a shopping edge, and those who master the art of bargaining (limited mostly to the markets) will have their purchasing power increased even more.

Gift Ideas

The flea markets in Acapulco carry what seems to be an inexhaustible supply of inexpensive collectibles and souvenirs, including serapes, ceramics, straw hats, shell sculptures, carved walking canes, and wooden toys. The selections of archaeological artifact replicas, bamboo wind chimes, painted wooden birds (from $5 to $100 each), shell earrings, and embroidered clothes begin to look identical. Prices at the flea markets are often quite low, but it's a good idea to compare prices of items you're interested in with prices in the shops, and bargaining is essential. It's best to buy articles described as being made from semiprecious stones or silver in reputable establishments. If you don't, you may find that the beautiful jade or lapis lazuli that was such a bargain was really cleverly painted paste, or that the silver was simply a facsimile called *alpaca*. Real sterling should always be stamped with the "sterling" or .925 hallmark. The large AFA (Artesanías Finas de Acapulco) crafts shop, though, has fixed prices and will ship, so this is the place to purchase onyx lamp stands and other larger items (*see* Food and Flea Markets, *below*). Clothes are another reasonably priced gift item. There are a couple of fashionable boutiques that sell designer clothes, but the majority of shops stock cotton sportswear and casual resort clothes. Made-to-order clothes are well made and especially reasonable. Otherwise be careful, since quality is not high and many goods self-destruct a few months after you get back home.

Shopping Districts

The main shopping strip is from the Acapulco Plaza to the El Presidente Hotel and is where you can find Benetton, Peer, Aca Joe, Look, Rubén Torres, Fiorucci, and others. Downtown (Old) Acapulco doesn't have many name shops, but this is where you'll find the inexpensive tailors patronized by the Mexicans, lots of little souvenir shops, and the flea market with crafts made for tourists. The tailors are all on Calle Benito Juárez, just west of the zócalo. Also downtown are Woolworth's and Sanborns.

Food and Flea Markets

The **Mercado Municipal** is described in Chapter 3, Exploring.

El Mercado de Artesanías is a 20-minute walk from the zócalo. Turn left as you leave Woolworth's and head straight until you reach the Multibanco Comermex. Turn right for one block and then turn left. When you reach the Banamex, the market is on your right. The market itself is a conglomeration of every souvenir in town: fake tribal masks, the ever-present onyx chessboards, the $25 hand-embroidered dresses, imitation silver, hammocks, ceramics, even skin cream made from turtles. (Don't buy it, because turtles are endangered and you won't get it through U.S. Customs.) The market is open daily 9–9. If you don't want to make the trip downtown, try **Noa Noa** on the Costera at Calle Hurtado de Mendoza. It's a cleaner, more commercial version of the Mercado Municipal and has T-shirts and jewelry, as well as the dozens of souvenirs available in the other markets.

Artesanías Finas de Acapulco (AFA) is one block north of the Costera behind the Baby O disco. All the souvenirs you have seen in town and lots more are available in 13,000 square feet of air-conditioned shopping space. AFA also carries household items, complete sets of dishes, suitcases, leather goods, and conservative clothing, as well as fashionable shorts and T-shirts. The staff is helpful. AFA ships to the United States and accepts major credit cards.

Two blocks west of the zócalo is **Calle José M. Iglesia,** home to a row of little souvenir shops that have a smaller selection than the big markets but many more T-shirts and more shell sculptures, shell ashtrays, and shell key chains than you ever imagined possible.

Art

Contemporary Art Gallery, at the Hyatt Regency, carries the work of contemporary Mexican artists, including Leonardo Nierman, as well as handicrafts that almost border on art. *Open Mon.–Sat. 10–8.*

Galería Rudic, across from the Continental Plaza, is one of the best galleries in town, with a good collection of top contemporary Mexican artists, including Armando Amaya, Leonardo Nierman, Norma Goldberg, Trinidad Osorio, José Clemente Orozco, and José David Alfaro Siqueiros. *Open weekdays 10–2 and 5–8.*

Galería Victor recently moved from its familiar location across from the Continental and is now at Plaza Bahía. On display is the work of the late Victor Salmones. *Open 10–2 and 4–8. Closed Sun.*

The sculptor **Pal Kepenyes** continues to receive good press. His jewelry is available in the Hyatt Regency arcade. It's also on display in his house at Guitarrón 140. Good luck with his perennially busy phone number, tel. 74/84-37-38.

Sergio Bustamente's whimsical painted papier-mâché and giant ceramic sculptures can be seen at the Princess Hotel shopping arcade and at his own gallery (Costera Miguel Alemán 711-B, next to American Express).

Boutiques

The mall section (*see below*) lists clothing shops, but there are several places strung along the Costera (mainly between the El Presidente and Fiesta Americana hotels), that are noteworthy. **Mad Max** has tasteful cotton separates in bold colors for children and shirts sporting the shop's logo (all about $25). **Aca Joe, Rubén Torres, Polo Ralph Lauren, Benetton,** and **OP** are scattered around the Costera, too. Sold at No. 143, the **Maria de Guadalajara** line of comfortable casual clothes for women is made from crinkly cotton in subdued and pastel colors. There are also a few high-fashion boutiques that will make clothes to order, and many can alter clothes to suit you, so it is always worth asking.

Nautica, in the Galería Plaza, is a boutique stocked with stylish casual clothing for men.

In Plaza Bahía, **Marithé and François Girbaud** carry a selection of very stylish casuals, designed in France and made in Mexico for men and women.

Marietta is located on the Costera at the Torre de Acapulco. It has a large collection that ranges from simple daywear to extravagantly sexy party dresses. This is a standby for expatriates in Acapulco. Though the clothes may seem expensive (cotton dresses from $70 to $150), they are quite a bit cheaper than they would be in the United States. The store also has a good selection of men's shirts.

Pit, located in the Princess arcade, is another bonanza. It carries a smashing line of beach cover-ups and hand-painted straw hats, as well as bathing suits and light dresses.

Custom-made Clothes The most famous of the made-to-order boutiques is **Samy's** at Calle Hidalgo 7, two blocks west of the zócalo, a crammed little shop next to a florist. It boasts a clientele of international celebrities and many of the important local families. Samy, the charming owner, takes all customers to heart and treats them like old, much-loved friends. He makes clothes for men and women, all in light cottons. The patterns are unusual and heavily influenced by Mexican designs, with embroidery and gauze playing a supporting role in the Samy look. The outfits are appropriate for trendy over-30s. Anything that doesn't fit can be altered, and Samy will even work with fabric that you bring in. Prices start at about $30. There is also a ready-to-wear line.

Esteban's, the most glamorous shop in Acapulco, is on the Costera near the Club de Tennis and

Golf. Like Samy, Esteban will make clothes to order and adapt anything you see in the shop. The similarity ends there, however. Esteban's clothes are far more formal and fashionable. His opulent evening dresses range from $200 to $1,000, though daytime dresses average $120. If you scour the racks, you can find something for $100. The real bargains are on the second floor, where some items are marked down as much as 80%. Esteban has a back room filled with designer clothes.

Benny, known for years for his custom-designed resortwear for men, now caters to women as well. He has two shops on the Costera, one across from the Torres Gemelas condominiums and another across from the El Presidente. A third shop is located downtown at Ignacio de la Llave 2, local 10.

Jewelry

Aha, in Plaza Bahía, has the most unusual costume jewelry in Acapulco. Designed by owner Cecilia Rodriguez, this is really campy, colorful stuff that is bound to attract attention. Prices range from $12 to $300.

Emi Fors (Galería Plaza and the Continental Plaza) are tony jewelry shops owned by Mrs. Fors, a former Los Angelina. The stores stock gold, silver, and some semiprecious stones.

Arles, at the Galería Acapulco Plaza, carries the beautiful Oro de Monte Alban collection of gold replicas of Oaxacan artifacts, as well as watches, handicrafts, and handpainted tin soldiers.

Antoinette, at the Acapulco Princess shopping arcade, has gold jewelry of impeccable design, set with precious and semiprecious stones, as well as a surprisingly uninspired display of silver items.

Silver

Many people come to Mexico to buy silver. Taxco, three hours away, is one of the silver capitals of the world (*see* Chapter 9, Excursions from Acapulco). Prices in Acapulco are lower than those in the United States but not dirt-cheap by any means. Bangles start at $8 and go up to $20; bracelets range from $20 to $100. Just look for the .925 sterling silver hallmark, or buy the more inexpensive silver plate that is dipped in several coats (*baños*) of silver. **Miguel Pineda** and **Los Castillo** are two of the more famous design names. Designs range from traditional bulky necklaces (often made with turquoise) to streamlined bangles and chunky earrings. Not much flatware can be found, although Emi Fors and Tane (*see below*) do carry some.

Tane (Hyatt Regency and Las Brisas hotels) carries small selections of the exquisite flatware, jewelry, and objets d'art created by one of Mexico's most prestigious (and expensive) silversmiths.

La Joya (Acapulco Plaza) stocks a good collection of inexpensive silver jewelry in modern designs and an extensive array of low-priced bangles (in the $6 range). Joya sells wholesale and will give a 30% discount on every item. *Open weekdays 9–6, Sat. 9–5.*

Malls

Malls are all the rage in Acapulco, and new ones are constantly being built. These range from the lavish air-conditioned shopping arcade at the Princess to rather gloomy collections of shops that sell cheap jewelry and embroidered dresses. Malls are listed below from east to west.

The cool arcade of the **Princess** is one of Acapulco's classiest, most comfortable malls. Serious shopping takes place here. Best bets are quality jewelry, clothes, leather, accessories, and artwork. Even if you are staying on the Costera, it is worth the cab ride out here just to see the shops.

Across from the Fiesta Americana Condesa Hotel is the **Plaza Condesa,** which offers a cold-drink stand, an Italian restaurant, a weight-training center, and a greater concentration of silver shops than you'll find anywhere else in Acapulco. Next door to Plaza Condesa is a high-tech, two-story building with a gym, OP for trendy sportswear, Rubén Torres, Acapulco

Joe, and Mad Max. The multilevel **Marbella Mall,** at the Diana Glorieta, has Peletier Paris jewelers and Bing's Ice Cream, as well as several restaurants. **Aca Mall,** which is on the other side of the Diana Glorieta, is all white and marble. Here you'll find Polo Ralph Lauren, Esprit, Ferrioni, Aca Joe, Express, and Marti (which carries a huge variety of sports equipment).

Plaza Bahía, next to the Acapulco Plaza, is a huge, completely enclosed and air-conditioned mall where you could easily spend an entire day. Here you'll find Calvin Klein; Docker's; Esprit; Fiorucci; Marithé and François Girbaud; Nautica; Benetton; Aspasia, which carries a line of locally designed glitzy evening dresses and chunky diamanté jewelry; Bally and Domit, for shoes; Armando's Girasol, with its distinctive line of women's clothing; restaurants and snack bars; Marti; and a video-games arcade. Bazar Bahía, on the second floor, has a fairly unusual selection of Mexican crafts. The list goes on and on.

Galería Plaza, which is looking somewhat seedy, is a two-story structure of air-conditioned shops built around a courtyard. Except for the silver, you could find many similar items at home. But this is a good place for picking up cotton sportswear or a pretty dress to wear to a disco. Arles, upstairs, has an interesting display of lead soldiers and a stunning collection of copies of pre-Hispanic gold jewelry found in a tomb at Monte Alban in Oaxaca. Guess! is one block west as you leave the plaza. Across from the Galería Plaza is the **Flamboyant Mall.**

Department Stores

Sanborns is the most un-Mexican of the big shops. It sells English-language newspapers, magazines, and books, as well as a line of high-priced souvenirs, but its Mexican glassware and ceramics cannot be found anywhere else in town. This is a useful place to come for postcards, cosmetics, and medicines. Sanborns's restaurants are recommended for glorified coffee-shop food. *The branch adjacent to the Condesa, Costera Miguel Alemán 209, is open* *until 1 AM; the downtown branch, Costera Miguel Alemán 1206, closes at 10:30 PM.*

Two branches of **Aurrerá** and **Gigante,** all on the Costera, and the **Super Super** downtown sell everything from light bulbs and newspapers to bottles of tequila and postcards. If you are missing anything at all, you should be able to pick it up at either of these stores or at the **Comercial Mexicana,** a store a little closer to the Costera. *Open until 9 PM.*

Woolworth's, at the corner of Escudero and Matamoros streets in Old Acapulco, is much like the five-and-dime stores found all over the United States but with a Mexican feel. There are also several mini-Woolworth's along the Costera. *Open until 9 PM.*

5 Sports and Fitness

Participant Sports and Fitness

Acapulco has lots for sports lovers to enjoy. Most hotels have pools, and there are several tennis courts on the Costera. The weight-training craze has caught on, and gyms are opening. You'll find one at Plaza Condesa across from the Fiesta Americana Condesa Hotel.

Fishing Sailfish, marlin, shark, and mahimahi are the usual catches. Head down to the docks near the zócalo and see just how many people offer to take you out for $30 a day. It is safer to stick with one of the reliable companies whose boats and equipment are in good condition.

Fishing trips can be arranged through your hotel, downtown at the Pesca Deportiva near the *muelle* (dock) across from the zócalo, or through travel agents. Boats accommodating 4 to 10 people cost $180–$500 a day, $45 to $60 by the chair. Excursions usually leave about 7 AM and return at 1 or 2 PM. You are required to get a license ($7) from the Secretaría de Pesca above the central post office downtown, but most fishing outfits take care of this. Don't show up during siesta, between 2 and 4 in the afternoon. For deep-sea fishing, **Arnold Brothers** (Costera Miguel Alemán 205, tel. 74/82–18–77) has well-maintained boats for five passengers (four lines). Small boats for freshwater fishing can be rented at **Cadena's** and **Tres Marías** at Coyuca lagoon. **Divers de México** (*see* Scuba Diving, *below*) rents chairs on fishing boats for about $55 per person.

Fitness and Swimming Acapulco weather is like August in the warmest parts of the United States. This means that you should cut back on your workouts and maintain proper hydration by drinking plenty of water.

Acapulco Princess Hotel (Carretera Escénica, Km 17, tel. 74/69–10–00) offers the best fitness facilities, with five pools, 11 tennis courts, and a gym with stationary bikes, Universal machines, and free weights. Because the Princess is about 15 kilometers (9 miles) from the city center, you can even swim in the ocean here, avoiding the pollution of Acapulco Bay. Beware: The waves are rough and the undertow is strong.

Villa Vera Spa and Fitness Center (Lomas del Mar 35, tel. 74/84–03–33) has a modern spa and fitness center and is equipped with exercise machines (including step machines), free weights, and benches. Masseuses and cosmetologists give facials and massages inside or by the pool, as you wish. Both the beauty center and the gym are open to nonguests.

Westin Las Brisas (Carretera Escénica 5255, tel. 74/84–15–80) is where you should stay if you like to swim but don't like company or competition. Individual casitas come with private, or semi-private, pools; the beach club has two saltwater pools, a Home Fitness System, and workout machines.

Most of the major hotels in town along the Costera Miguel Alemán also have pools.

Golf There are two 18-hole championship golf courses shared by the Princess and Pierre Marqués hotels. Reservations should be made in advance (tel. 74/84–31–00). Greens fees are $68 for guests and $90 for nonguests. There is also a public golf course at the Club de Tennis and Golf (tel. 74/84–07–81) on the Costera across from the Acapulco Malibu hotel. Greens fees are $27 for nine holes, $40 for 18 holes.

Jogging The only real venue for running in the downtown area is along the sidewalk next to the seafront Costera Miguel Alemán. Early morning is the best time, since traffic is heavy along this thoroughfare during most of the day and the exhaust fumes can make running unpleasant. The sidewalk measures close to 8 kilometers (5 miles). The beach is another option, but as with beaches everywhere, the going is tough, with soft sand and sloping contours. Away from the city center, the best area for running is out at the Acapulco Princess Hotel, on the airport road. A 2-kilometer (1.2-mile) loop is laid out along a lightly traveled road, and in the early morning you can also run along the asphalt trails on the golf course.

Scuba Diving **Divers de México** (tel. 74/82–13–98), owned by a helpful and efficient American woman, provides English-speaking captains and comfortable American-built yachts. A three- to four-hour scuba-diving excursion, including equipment, lessons in a pool for beginners, and drinks, costs

about $52 per person. If you are a certified div-
er, the excursion is $45.

Arnold Brothers (*see* Fishing, *above*) also runs
daily scuba-diving excursions and snorkeling
trips. The scuba trips cost $35 and last for 2½
hours.

Tennis Court fees range from about $5 to $20 an hour
during the day and are $3–$5 more in the evening. Nonhotel guests pay about $5 more per
hour. Lessons, with English-speaking instruc-
tors, are about $25 an hour; ball boys get a $2 tip.
Following is a list of places to play.

Acapulco Plaza, three hard-surface courts, two
lighted for evening play (tel. 74/84–90–50). **Acapulco Princess,** two indoor courts, nine outdoor
(tel. 74/84–31–00). **Club de Tennis and Golf,**
across from Hotel Malibu, Costera Miguel Alemán (tel. 74/84–07–81). **Hyatt Regency,** five
lighted courts (tel. 74/84–12–25). **Pierre
Marqués,** five courts (tel. 74/84–20–00).
Tiffany's Racquet Club, Avenue Villa Vera 120,
five courts (tel. 74/84–79–49). **Villa Vera Hotel,**
three outdoor lighted clay courts (tel. 74/84–
02–24).

Water Sports Waterskiing, broncos (one-person motorboats),
and parasailing can all be arranged on the
beach. Parasailing is an Acapulco highlight and
looks terrifying until you actually try it. Most
people who do it love the view and go back again
and again. An eight-minute trip costs $15 (tel.
74/82–20–56). Waterskiing is about $20 a half-
hour; broncos cost $30 for a half-hour.
Windsurfing can be arranged at Caleta and most
of the beaches along the Costera but is especially good at Puerto Marqués. At Coyuca Lagoon,
you can try your hand (or feet) at barefoot
waterskiing. The main surfing beach is
Revolcadero.

Spectator Sports

Bullfights The season runs from Christmas to Easter, and
corridas are held—sporadically—on Sundays
at 5:30. Tickets are available through your hotel
or at the Plaza de Toros ticket window (Av. Cir-
cunvalación, across from Caleta Beach, tel. 74/
82–11–81); open Mon.–Sat. 10–2 and Sun.

10:30–3. Tickets cost from $20 to $25, and a $25 seat in the first four rows—in the shade (*sombra*)—is worth the extra cost. Also check the local paper and signs around town to find out if any noteworthy matadors can be seen in action.

Beaches

The lure of sun and sand in Acapulco is legendary. Every sport is available, and you can shop from roving souvenir vendors, eat in a beach restaurant, dance, and sleep in a *hamaca* (hammock) without leaving the water's edge. If you want to avoid the crowds, there are also plenty of quiet and even isolated beaches within reach. However, some of these, such as Revolcadero and Pie de la Cuesta, have very strong undertows and surfs, so swimming is not advised. Despite an enticing appearance and claims that officials are cleaning up the bay, it remains polluted. If this bothers you, we suggest that you follow the lead of the Mexican cognoscenti and take the waters at your hotel pool.

Beaches in Mexico are public, even those that seem to belong to a big hotel. The list below moves from east to west.

Barra Vieja   About 27 kilometers (16 miles) east of Acapulco, between Laguna de Tres Palos and the Pacific, this magnificent beach is even more inviting than Pie de la Cuesta (*see below*) because you're not bothered by itinerant peddlers and beggars; the drive there is also more pleasant.

Revolcadero   A wide, sprawling beach next to the Pierre Marqués and Princess hotels, its water is shallow and its waves are fairly rough. People come here to surf and ride horses.

Puerto Marqués   Tucked below the airport highway, this strand is popular with Mexican tourists, so it tends to get crowded on weekends.

Icacos   Stretching from the naval base to El Presidente, this beach is less populated than others on the Castera. The morning waves are especially calm.

Condesa Facing the middle of Acapulco Bay, this stretch of sand has more than its share of tourists, especially singles. The beachside restaurants are convenient for bites between parasailing flights.

Hornos and Running from the Paraíso Radisson to Las
Hornitos Hamacas hotel, these beaches are packed shoulder to shoulder with Mexican tourists. These tourists know a good thing: Graceful palms shade the sand, and there are scads of casual eateries within walking distance.

Caleta and On the peninsula in Old Acapulco, these two
Caletilla beaches once rivaled La Quebrada as the main tourist area in Acapulco's heyday. Now they attract families. Motorboats to Roqueta leave from here.

Roqueta A ferry costs about $6 round-trip, including en-
Island trance to the zoo; the trip takes 10 minutes each way. Acapulqueños consider Roqueta Island their day-trip spot.

Pie de la You'll need a car or cab to reach this relatively
Cuesta unpopulated spot, about 15 minutes west of town. A few rustic restaurants border the wide beach, and straw palapas provide shade.

6 Dining

Dining in Acapulco is more than just eating out—it is the most popular leisure activity in town. Every night the restaurants fill up, and every night the adventurous diner can sample a different cuisine: Italian, German, Japanese, American, Tex-Mex, and, of course, plain old Mex. The variety of styles matches the range of cuisines: from greasy spoons that serve regional specialties to rooftop gourmet restaurants with gorgeous views of Acapulco Bay. Most restaurants fall somewhere in the middle, and on the Costera there are dozens of beachside restaurants, roofed with palapa (palm frond), as well as wildly decorated rib and hamburger joints popular with visitors under 30.

One plus for Acapulco dining is that the food is garden fresh. Each morning the Mercado Municipal is abuzz with restaurant managers and locals buying up the vegetables that will appear on plates that evening. Although some top-quality beef is now being produced in the states of Sonora and Chihuahua, many of the more expensive restaurants claim that they import their beef from the States. Whether or not they're telling the truth, the beef is excellent in most places. Establishments that cater to tourists purify their drinking water and use it to cook vegetables. In smaller restaurants, ask for bottled water with or without bubbles (*con* or *sin gas*).

The top restaurants in Acapulco can be fun for a splurge and provide very good value. Even at the best places in town, dinner rarely exceeds $45 per person, and the atmosphere and views are fantastic. Ties and jackets are out of place, but so are shorts or jeans. Unless stated otherwise, all restaurants are open daily from 6:30 or 7 PM until the last diner leaves. Several restaurants have two seatings: 6:30 for the *gringos* and 9 for the Mexican crowd, who wisely head directly for the discos after dinner to dance off the calories.

A word on hygiene: Most travelers to Mexico are only too familiar with the caveat "Don't drink the water" (*see* Staying Healthy, in Chapter 1). Again, stick to bottled waters and soft drinks, and when ordering cold drinks at untouristed establishments, skip the ice *(sin hielo)*. (You can usually identify ice made commercially from purified water by its uniform shape and the hole in the center.) Hotels with water purification systems will post signs to that effect in the rooms. *Tacos al pastor*—thin pork slices grilled on a spit and garnished with the usual cilantro, onions, and chile—are delicious but dangerous. Be wary of Mexican hamburgers, because you can never be certain what meat they are made with (horsemeat is very common).

Highly recommended restaurants are indicated by a star ★.

Category	Cost*
$$$$	over $35
$$$	$25–$35
$$	$15–$25
$	under $15

per person, excluding drinks, service, and sales tax (10%)

Continental
$$$$

Bella Vista. This alfresco restaurant in the exclusive Las Brisas area has fantastic sunset views of Acapulco. Its large menu offers a wide variety of dishes that range from Asian appetizers to Italian and seafood entrées. Try the delicious (and spicy!) Thai shrimp, sautéed in sesame oil, ginger, Thai chili, and hoisin sauce, or the red snapper Etouffée, cooked in chardonnay, tomato, herbs, basil and oyster sauce. *Carretera Escéncia 5255, tel. 74/84–15–80, ext. 500. Reservations required. AE, DC, MC, V.*

$$$$
★

Coyuca 22. This is possibly the most expensive restaurant in Acapulco; it is certainly one of the most beautiful. Diners eat on terraces that overlook the bay from the west, on a hilltop in Old Acapulco. The understated decor consists of Doric pillars, sculptures, and large onyx flower stands near the entrance. Diners gaze down on an enormous illuminated obelisk and a small pool. The effect is that of eating in a partially restored Greek ruin sans dust. The tiny menu cen-

Acapulco Dining

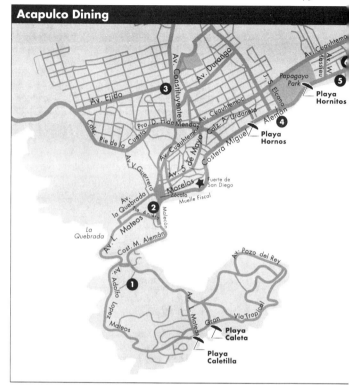

Acapulco Fat Farm, **2**

Belle Vista, **24**

Beto's, **10**

Blackbeard's, **9**

Carlos 'n Charlies, **11**

Casa Nova, **23**

Casimiro's, **18**

Coyuca 22, **1**

D'Joint, **13**

El Cabrito, **15**

Embarcadero, **16**

Hard Rock Café, **14**

Hard Times, **12**

Le Gourmat, **25**

Los Rancheros, **20**

Madeiras, **22**

Mimi's Chili Saloon, **8**

Miramar, **21**

100% Natural, **6**

Paradise, **7**

Sirocco, **4**

Suntory, **17**

Tlaquepaque, **3**

Zapata Villa y Cia., **19**

Zorrito's , **5**

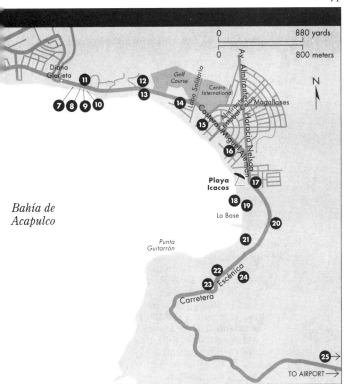

0   880 yards

0   800 meters

N

Diana
Glorieta

11

7 **8** **9** **10**

12

13

Golf
Course

Lobo Solitario

Centro
Internacional

Av. Almirante Jo

14

Costera Miguel Alemán

Escudero Magallanes

Horacio Nelson

15

16

**Playa
Icacos**

17

18 **19**

La Base

20

*Bahía de
Acapulco*

21

Punta
Guitarrón

22

23

24

Escénica

Carretera

25 →

TO AIRPORT →

ters on seafood, with lobster the house specialty. Prime rib is also available. *Avenida Coyuca 22 (a 10-min taxi ride from the zócalo), tel. 74/82–34–68 or 74/83–50–30. Reservations required. AE, DC, MC, V. Closed Apr. 30–Nov. 1.*

French **Le Gourmet.** Although its food is somewhat in-
$$$$ consistent, this restaurant is thought by many to be one of Acapulco's premier establishments. Many people staying down on the Costera brave the 15-minute taxi ride to partake of a tranquil meal in a plush setting. The French menu has all the classics: vichyssoise, steak au poivre sautéed in cognac, and such Acapulco favorites as lobster and red snapper fillets. The atmosphere is luxurious and genteel, with roomy, comfortable chairs, silent waiters, and air-conditioning. *Acapulco Princess Hotel, tel. 74/84–31–00. Reservations advised. AE, DC, MC, V.*

Italian **Casa Nova.** Another ultraromantic spot created
$$$$ by Arturo Cordova, the man behind Coyuca 22
★ *(see above),* Casa Nova is carved out of a cliff that rises up from Acapulco Bay. The views, both from the terrace and the air-conditioned interior dining room, are spectacular, the service impeccable, and the Italian cuisine divine. The menu includes antipasto, fresh pastas, a delightful *cotolette de vittello* (veal chops with mushrooms), lobster tail, and *linguini alle vongole* (linguini with clams, tomato, and garlic). *Scenic Highway, just past Madeiras, tel. 74/84–68–19. Reservations required. AE, DC, MC, V.*

Japanese **Suntory.** At this traditional Japanese restau-
$$$$ rant you can dine either in a blessedly air-conditioned interior room or in the delightful Oriental-style garden. It's one of the few Japanese restaurants in Acapulco and also one of the only deluxe restaurants that is open for lunch. Specialties are the sushi and the teppan-yaki, prepared at your table by skilled chefs. *Suntory, Costera Miguel Alemán 36, across from the La Palapa hotel, tel. 74/84–80–88. Reservations advised for dinner only. AE, DC, MC, V.*

Seafood **Blackbeard's.** A dark, glorified coffee shop with
$$$$ a pirate-ship motif, Blackbeard's—owned by the proprietors of Mimi's Chili Saloon *(see be-*

low)—has maps covering the tables in the cozy booths, and the walls are adorned with wooden figureheads. Every movie star, from Bing Crosby to Liz Taylor, who ever set foot here has his or her photo posted in the lounge. A luscious salad bar and jumbo portions of shrimp, steak, and lobster keep customers satisfied. A disco on the premises starts throbbing at 10:30 PM. *Costera Miguel Alemán, tel. 74/84–25–49. Reservations advised. AE, DC, MC, V.*

American
$$$
★
Carlos 'n' Charlie's. This is without a doubt the most popular restaurant in town; a line forms well before the 6:30 PM opening. Part of the Anderson group (with restaurants in the United States and Spain as well as Mexico), Carlos 'n' Charlie's cultivates an atmosphere of controlled craziness. Prankster waiters, a jokester menu, and eclectic decor—everything from antique bullfight photos to a tool chest of painted gadgets hanging from the ceiling—add to the chaos. The menu straddles the border, with ribs, stuffed shrimp, and oysters among the best offerings. *Costera Miguel Alemán 999, tel. 74/84–12–85 or 84–00–39. No reservations. AE, DC, MC, V.*

$$$
Embarcadero. A nautical motif pervades Embarcadero, which is well loved by both Acapulco regulars and resident Americans. It is designed to look like a wharf with the bar as the loading office. Wooden bridges lead past a fountain to the thatched eating area, piled high with wooden packing crates and maps. The food is American with a Polynesian touch. You can have deep-fried shrimp with garlic sauce, tempura, chicken, or steak. The "salad barge" is enormous. *Costera Miguel Alemán, southeast of CiCi Park, tel. 74/84–87–87. Open 6 PM–midnight. No reservations. AE, DC, MC, V. Closed Mon. out of season.*

$$$
★
Hard Rock Cafe. A bar, restaurant, and dance hall filled with rock memorabilia, this link in the international Hard Rock chain is one of the most popular spots in Acapulco, and with good reason. The southern-style food—fried chicken, ribs, chili con carne—is very well prepared and the portions are more than ample. The taped rock music begins at noon, and a live group starts playing at 11 PM. There's always a line at

the small boutique on the premises where you can buy sports clothes and accessories bearing the Hard Rock label. *Costera Miguel Alemán 37, tel. 74/84-66-80. Reservations advised. AE, MC, V.*

Continental
$$$
★

Madeiras. This place is very difficult to get into, especially on weekends and during the Christmas and Easter holidays; many people make reservations by letter before their arrival. The furniture is certainly unusual: The bar-reception area has art nouveau–style carved chairs, plump sofas, and startling coffee tables made of glass resting on large wooden animals. All the dishes and silverware were created by silversmiths in the nearby town of Taxco. Dinner is served from a four-course, prix fixe menu and costs about $32 without wine. Entrées include the delicious Spanish dish of red snapper in sea salt, tasty chilled soups, stuffed red snapper, and a choice of steaks and other seafood. *Scenic Highway just past La Vista shopping center, tel. 74/84-73-16. Reservations required. AE, DC, MC, V.*

French
$$$
★

Miramar. Light-wood furniture and a fountain provide the decoration for this understated place, but the real glamour comes from the view of the bay and the flickering lights of Acapulco. Traditional dishes, such as pâté and lobster thermidor, are served alongside classics with a new twist: ceviche with a hint of coconut and red snapper papillote. Smoked salmon, smoked oyster mousse, and duck are all specialties. Miramar is not as intimate as its neighbor, Madeiras, and many large groups from the Princess book long tables, so the noise level is rather high. *Scenic Highway at La Vista shopping center, tel. 74/84-78-74. Reservations advised. AE, DC, MC, V. Closed Sept.–Oct.*

Mexican
$$$

Zapata, Villa y Cia. This is a Mexican version of the Hard Rock Cafe, where the music and food (excellent) are strictly Mexican and the memorabilia is Mexican Revolution, with guns, hats, and photographs of Pancho Villa. The definite highlight of an evening here is a visit from a sombrero-wearing baby burro, so be sure to bring your camera. *Hyatt Regency, Costera Miguel*

Alemán 1, tel. 74/84–28–88. No reservations. AE, DC, MC, V.

American **D'Joint.** Locals as well as tourists love
$$ D'Joint—a claustrophobic restaurant with a
funky, publike atmosphere and a popular sports
bar—so, in season, prepare for a wait. In addi-
tion to the usual steaks, salads, and nachos,
prime rib is the house specialty. The four types
of roast beef sandwiches are another hit. After
your meal, try "sexy coffee"—cappuccino with
liqueur. *Costera Miguel Alemán 79, next door to
the Hotel Acapulco Malibu, tel. 74/84–19–13.
No reservations. AE, DC, MC, V. Closed 1 wk
in summer.*

$$ **Hard Times.** With an unusually large menu for
★ Acapulco, Hard Times features the usual Tex-
Mex dishes as well as plenty of barbecue, fresh
fish, and the largest salad bar in town. The dining area is an attractive open terrace, with a
partial view of the bay. Although it is right in
the center of the Costera, Hard Times is a tranquil haven—decorated with palms and incan-
descent lights—in which to enjoy generous
portions of American food and, sometimes, jazz.
Arrive early; there is often a wait in high season. *Costera Miguel Alemán, across from the
Calinda Quality Hotel (look for the red neon
lights), tel. 74/84–00–64. Reservations advised
during high season. AE, DC, MC, V. Closed
Sun. during summer.*

Mexican **Los Rancheros.** With a view of the water in the
$$ posh East Bay, here's Mexican food at about half
what you'd pay at Madeiras or Miramar. The de-
cor is colorful, folksy Mexican with paper
streamers, checked tablecloths, and lopsided
mannequins in local dress. Specials include
carne tampiqueña (fillet of beef broiled with
lemon juice), chicken enchiladas, and *queso
fundido* (melted cheese served as a side dish
with chips). There is live music daily noon to
midnight. *Scenic Highway just before Extasis
disco (on the left as you head toward the air-
port), tel. 74/84–19–08. MC, V.*

Seafood **Paradise.** This is the leading beach-party res-
$$ taurant. T-shirted waiters drop leis over your
head as you arrive and hand roses to the ladies.
The menu (primarily seafood) has the same
number of dishes as drinks, a pretty good indi-

cator of what this place is like. Paradise has one of the biggest dance floors in Acapulco and live music day and night. Chaos reigns at lunchtime (from 2 to 5), and the mood picks up again from 8:30 to 10:30. Expect a young crowd. *Costera Miguel Alemán 107, next to Mimi's Chili Saloon, tel. 74/84–59–88. No reservations. AE, DC, MC, V.*

Spanish **Sirocco.** This beachside eatery is numero uno for
$$ those who crave Spanish food in Acapulco. The tiled floors and heavy wooden furniture give it a Mediterranean feel. Specialties include *pulpo en su tinta* (octopus in its own ink) and 10 varieties of fresh fish. Order paella when you arrive at the beach—it takes a half hour to prepare. *Costera Miguel Alemán, across from Aurrerá, tel. 74/85–23–86 or 74/85–94–90. Reservations not required. AE, MC, V. Open 2–10 PM.*

Health Food **100% Natural.** Six family-operated restaurants
$ specialize in light, healthful food—yogurt
★ shakes, fruit salads, and sandwiches made with whole-wheat bread. The service is quick and the food is a refreshing alternative to tacos, particularly on a hot day. Look for the green signs with white lettering. *Costera Miguel Alemán 204, near the Acapulco Plaza, tel. 74/85–39–82. Another branch is at the Casa de la Cultura, tel. 74/81–08–44. No credit cards.*

$ **Zorrito's.** The old Zorrito's, a rather dingy but
★ popular café, is no longer, but a new, very clean restaurant of the same name is now attracting tourists. The menu features a host of steak and beef dishes, and the special, *filete tampiqueña*, comes with tacos, enchiladas, guacamole, and frijoles. *Costera Miguel Alemán and Anton de Alaminos, next to Banamex, tel. 74/85–37–35. No reservations. AE, MC, V. Open 9 AM–6 AM.*

Mexican **Casimiro's.** The specialty at this beachfront res-
$ taurant is seafood, but it is also a good source for some generic yet well-prepared Mexican dishes. *Icacos Beach, behind the Hyatt Regency, tel. 74/84–30–08. No reservations. AE, MC, V.*

El Cabrito. This is another local favorite for true Mexican cuisine and ambience. The name of the restaurant—"The Goat"—is also its specialty. In addition, you can choose among mole; jerky with egg, fish, and seafood; and other Mexican dishes. *Costera Miguel Alemán, between Nina's and Hard Rock, tel. 74/84–77–11. No reservations. MC, V.*

$ **Mimi's Chili Saloon.** Right next door to Paradise
★ is this two-level wooden restaurant decorated with everything from Marilyn Monroe posters to cages of tropical birds and a collection of ridiculous signs. It's frequented by those under (and frequently over) 30 who gorge on Tex-Mex, onion rings, and excellent burgers and wash them down with peach and mango daiquiris. Or the waiters will bring you anything on the menu next door at Blackbeard's. Be prepared for a wait in the evenings. *Costera Miguel Alemán, tel. 74/85–64–62. No reservations. AE, MC, V. Closed Mon. and Labor Day (May 1).*

$ **Tlaquepaque.** As hard to find as it is to pro-
★ nounce, this is one of the best restaurants in Acapulco. It's well worth the 15-minute cab ride into the northwestern residential section of Acapulco (tell your driver it is around the corner from where the Oficina de Tránsito used to be). The alfresco dining area sits on a stone terrace bordered by pink flowering bushes and an abandoned well. The outside tables have a perfect view of the kitchen filled with locally made pots. Thursday is *pozole* day, when a thick soup of hominy and pork is served. *Calle Uno, Lote 7, Colonia Vista Alegre, tel. 74/85–70–55. Reservations advised on Thurs. (pozole day). Closed Mon. No credit cards.*

Mexican/ **Acapulco Fat Farm.** High-school and college stu-
American dents at the Acapulco Children's Home run this
$ cozy place in the center of town. The specialties include ice cream made with all natural ingredients, U.S.-style cakes and pies, sandwiches, hamburgers, and good Mexican food as well. The background music is classical, which is unusual for Acapulco, and there's an exhibition of paintings and masks as well as a book exchange. *Juárez 10, tel. 74/83–53–39. No reservations. No credit cards.*

Seafood **Beto's.** By day you can eat right on the beach
$ and enjoy live music; by night this palapa-roofed
★ restaurant is transformed into a dim and romantic dining area lighted by candles and paper lanterns. Whole red snapper, lobster, and ceviche are recommended. There is a second branch

next door and a third—where the specialty is *pescado a la talla* (fish spread with chili and other spices and then grilled over hot coals)—at **Barra Vieja Beach.** *Beto's, Costera Miguel Alemán, tel. 74/84–04–73. Beto's Safari, Costera Miguel Alemán, next to Beto's, tel. 74/84–47–62. Beto's Barra Vieja, Barra Vieja Beach, no phone. AE, MC, V.*

7 Lodging

Accommodations in Acapulco run the gamut
from sprawling, big-name complexes with nonstop amenities to small, family-run inns where
hot water is a luxury. Wherever you stay, however, prices will be reasonable compared with
those in the United States, and service is generally good, since Acapulqueños have been catering to tourists for more than 40 years.
Accommodations above $90 (double) are air-con-
ditioned (but you can find air-conditioned hotels
for less) and include a minibar, TV, and a view of
the bay. There is usually a range of in-house restaurants and bars, as well as a pool. Exceptions
exist, such as Las Brisas, which, in the name of
peace and quiet, has banned TVs from all rooms.
So if such extras are important to you, be sure to
ask ahead. If you can't afford air-conditioning,
don't panic. Even the cheapest hotels have cool-
ing ceiling fans.

Although Acapulco has been an important port
since colonial times, it lacks the converted mon-
asteries and old mansions found in Mexico City.
But the Costera is chockablock with new luxury
high rises and local franchises of such major
U.S. hotel chains as Hyatt and Howard John-
son. Since these hotels tend to be characterless,
your choice will depend on location and what facilities are available. Villa Vera, Acapulco Plaza, Las Brisas, and the Hyatt have tennis courts
as well as swimming pools. The Princess and
Pierre Marqués share two 18-hole golf courses,
and the Royal Elcano is across from the Club de
Tennis and Golf. All major hotels can make water-sports arrangements.

In Acapulco geography is price, so where you
stay determines what you pay. The most exclusive area is the Acapulco Diamante, home to
some of the most expensive hotels in Mexico—so
lush and well equipped that most guests don't
budge from the minute they arrive. The
minuses: Revolcadero Beach is too rough for
swimming (though great for surfing), and the
East Bay is a 15-minute (expensive) taxi ride
from the heart of Acapulco. There is also very
little to do in this area except play golf at the
Acapulco Princess, dine at three of Acapulco's
better restaurants (Madeiras, Casa Nova, and

Miramar), and dance at the glamorous Extravaganzza, Palladium, and Fantasy discos.

Americans tend to stay on Costera Miguel Alemán, where the majority of large hotels, discos,
American-style restaurants, and airline offices
may be found, along with Acapulco's best
beaches. All the Costera hotels have freshwater
pools and sundecks, and most have restaurants
and/or bars overlooking the beach, if not on the
sand itself. Hotels across the street are almost
always less expensive than those directly on the
beach; because there are no private beaches in
Acapulco, all you have to do is cross the road to
enjoy the sand.

Moving west along the Costera leads you to
downtown Acapulco, where the fishing and tour
boats depart and the locals go about their business. The central post office, Woolworth's, and
the Mercado Municipal are here, along with
countless restaurants where a complete meal
can cost as little as $5. The beaches here are pop-
ular with Mexican vacationers, and the dozens
of little hotels attract Canadian and European
bargain hunters.

Note: Most hotels are booked solid Christmas
and Easter week, so if you plan to visit then, it's
wise to make reservations months in advance.

Highly recommended hotels are indicated by a
star ★.

Category	Cost*
$$$$	over $160
$$$	$90–$160
$$	$40–$90
$	under $40

*All prices are for a standard double room, ex-
cluding 10% sales (called IVA) tax.*

Acapulco Diamante

$$$$ **Acapulco Princess.** A pyramid-shaped building
★ flanked by two towers, the Princess has the
largest capacity of any hotel in Acapulco. The

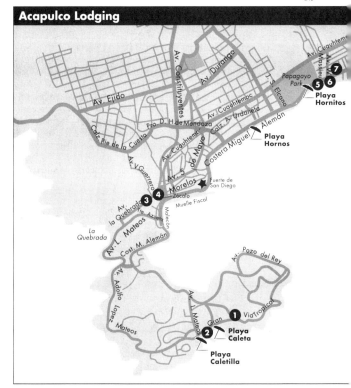

Acapulco Lodging

Acapulco
Plaza, **9**

Acapulco
Princess, **20**

Autotel Ritz, **7**

Boca Chica, **2**

Camino Real
Acapulco
Diamante, **21**

Copacabana, **15**

Fiesta
Americana
Condesa
Acapulco, **12**

Gran Motel
Acapulco, **10**

Hotel Acapulco
Tortuga, **11**

Hotel Misión, **3**

Hyatt Regency
Acapulco, **16**

Las Brisas, **18**

Maralisa
Hotel and
Beach Club , **8**

Paraíso
Radisson, **5**

Pierre
Marqués, **19**

Plaza las Glorias
El Mirador, **4**

Ritz, **6**

Royal
El Cano, **14**

Sheraton
Acapulco, **17**

Suites Alba, **1**

Villa Vera, **13**

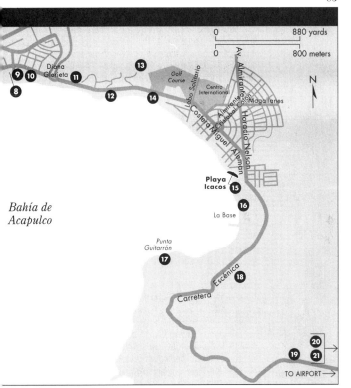

0
880 yards

0
800 meters

N

Av. Almirante o. Magallanes

Diana
Glorieta

9 **10**
8

11

13

Golf
Course

Centro
International

12

14

Lobo Solitario

Costera Miguel Alemán

Almirante Cristóbal

Horacio Nelson

*Bahía de
Acapulco*

**Playa
Icacos** **15**

16

La Base

Punta
Guitarrón

17

Carretera Escénica

18

20 →
19 **21**

TO AIRPORT →

hotel's fact sheet makes fascinating reading: 50 chocolate cakes are consumed daily and 2,500 staff meals are served. Rooms are light and airy, with cane furniture and crisp yellow-and-green rugs and curtains. Guests can also use the facilities of the hotel's smaller sibling, the Pierre Marqués; a free shuttle bus provides transport. Accommodations include breakfast and dinner (mandatory in high season). *Box 1351 Playa Revolcadero, 39907, tel. 74/69–10–00 or 800/ 223–1818. 1,019 balconied rooms, with bath. Facilities: two 18-hole golf courses, 11 tennis courts, 6 pools, 7 restaurants, 7 bars, disco, banquet rooms. AE, DC, MC, V.*

$$$$ **Camino Real Acapulco Diamante.** Opened in May 1993, Acapulco's newest hotel is set at the foot of a lush tropical hillside on exclusive Pichilingue beach, far from the madding crowd. All rooms are done in luscious pastels, with tiled floors, balcony or terrace, luxurious baths, ceiling fans, and air-conditioning. Each has a view of peaceful Puerto Marqués bay. *Playa Pichilingue, 39867, tel. 74/81–22–80 or 800/7– CAMINO. 153 rooms with ocean view, 2 terraced pools, tennis courts, fitness center, shopping arcade, restaurants, bars. AE, DC, MC, V.*

$$$$ **Las Brisas.** This self-contained luxury complex
★ covers 110 acres and has accommodations that range from one-bedroom units to deluxe private casitas, complete with private pools that are small yet swimmable. Everything at Las Brisas is splashed with pink, from the staff uniforms to the stripe up the middle of the road. Transportation is by white-and-pink Jeep. And transport is necessary—it is a good 15-minute walk to the beach restaurant, and all the facilities are far from the rooms. There are an art gallery and a few other stores. On Thursday there is a Jeep ranch safari, and Friday night is Cantina Night. Tipping is not allowed, but a service charge of $22 a day is added to the bill. The rate includes Continental breakfast. *Carretera Escénica 5255, 39868, tel. 74/84–15–80 or 800/228–3000, fax 74/84–22–69. 300 rooms with bath. Facilities: 4 restaurants, 2 bars, beach club, fitness machines, 2 saltwater pools, 1 freshwater pool, Jacuzzi and sauna, 5 lighted tennis courts, water sports, 2 conference rooms. AE, DC, MC, V.*

$$$$ **Pierre Marqués.** This hotel is doubly blessed: It
★ is closer to the beach than any of the other East
Bay hotels, and guests have access to all the
Princess's facilities without the crowds. In addition, it has three pools and five tennis courts illuminated for nighttime play. Rooms are
furnished identically to those at the Princess,
but duplex villas and bungalows with private
patios are available. Accommodations include
mandatory breakfast (breakfast and dinner during Christmas week). *Box 1351, Playa
Revolcadero, 39907, tel. 74/84–20–00 or 800/
223–1818. 334 rooms with bath. Facilities: two
18-hole golf courses, 5 lighted tennis courts, 3
pools, valet service, bar, 2 restaurants, shops.
Open only during the winter season. AE, DC,
MC, V.*

$$$ **Sheraton Acapulco.** Perfect for those who want
to enjoy the sun and the sand but don't have to
be in the center of everything, this Sheraton is
isolated from all the hubbub of the Costera and
is rather small in comparison with the chain's
other properties in Mexico. The rooms and
suites are distributed among 17 villas that are
set on a hillside on secluded Guitarrón Beach 10
kilometers (6 miles) east of Acapulco proper.
Rooms for the handicapped and nonsmokers are
available, and all units have private balconies
and a sweeping view of the entire bay. *Costera
Guitarrón 110, 39359, tel. 74/81–22–22 or 800/
325–3535. 198 rooms and 15 suites with bath.
Facilities: 2 pools, 3 restaurants, 3 bars, water
sports. AE, DC, MC, V.*

The Costera

$$$$ **Hyatt Regency Acapulco.** Another megahotel
that you never have to leave, this property is
popular with business travelers and convention-
eers. All the rooms are decorated in soft pastels
and should be completely refurbished by the
end of 1994. The Hyatt is a little out of the way, a
plus for those who seek quiet. Rooms on the
west side of the hotel are preferable for those
who want to avoid the noise of the maneuvers at
the neighboring naval base. *Costera Miguel
Alemán 1, 39869, tel. 74/84–28–88 or 800/223–
1234. 690 rooms with bath. Facilities: 5 tennis*

courts, pool, sauna and massage, shops, 4 restaurants, 5 bars, 6 conference rooms, parking. AE, DC, MC, V.

$$$$ **Royal El Cano.** One of Acapulco's traditional favorites has been completely remodeled, while still (thankfully) maintaining its '50s flavor. The interior decorators get an A+: The rooms are snappily done in white and navy blue, with white tiled floors and beautiful modern bathrooms. The only exception is the lobby, which is excruciatingly blue. There's a delightful outdoor restaurant, a more elegant indoor one, and a pool that seems to float above the bay with whirlpools built into the corners. *Costera Miguel Alemán 75, 39690, tel. 74/84–19–50. 340 rooms with bath. Facilities: 2 restaurants, bar, freshwater pool, banquet rooms. AE, DC, MC, V.*

$$$ **Acapulco Plaza.** This Holiday Inn resort is the largest and one of the newest hotels on the Costera. The Plaza Bahía next to the hotel is the largest shopping mall in town. The lobby bar is most extraordinary—a wooden hut, suspended by a cable from the roof, reached by a gangplank from the second floor of the lobby and overlooking a garden full of flamingos and other exotic birds. Guest rooms tell the same old story: pastels and blond wood replacing passé dark greens and browns. *Costera Miguel Alemán 123, 39670, tel. 74/85–80–50 or 800/HOLIDAY. 1,008 rooms with bath. Booked solid Dec. 20–Jan. 3. Facilities: health club, sauna, freshwater pools, 4 lighted tennis courts, water sports, 5 restaurants, 7 bars, conference rooms. AE, DC, MC, V.*

$$$ **Copacabana.** Here's a good buy if you yearn for a modern hotel in the center of things. The staff is efficient and helpful, the ambience relaxed and festive. The lobby and pool (with a swim-up bar) are always crowded with people enjoying themselves. The psychedelic pseudo-Mexican lemon-and-lime hues pervade the halls and bedrooms. *Tabachines 2, 39670, tel. 74/84–32–60 or 800/ 221–6509. 422 rooms, showers only. Facilities: pool, 2 restaurants, 2 bars, shops, conference rooms. AE, DC, MC, V.*

$$$ **Fiesta Americana Condesa Acapulco.** Right in ★ the thick of the main shopping-restaurant district, the Condesa, as everyone calls it, is ever popular with tour operators. However, in recent years rooms have become shabby and poorly maintained. Management has replaced the hotel's general director and promises that all rooms will be totally redecorated by the end of 1994, bringing the hotel back up to the high standards of the other Fiesta Americana properties. *Costera Miguel Alemán 1220, 39670, tel. 74/84–28–28 or 800/FIESTA–1. 500 rooms with bath. Facilities: 2 pools, water sports, 4 restaurants, bar, conference rooms. AE, DC, MC, V.*

$$$
★ **Paraíso Radisson.** The last of the big Costera hotels is a favorite of tour groups, so the lobby is forever busy. The rooms look brighter and roomier since the management replaced the heavy Spanish-style furniture with light woods and pastels. Guests lounge by the pool or at the beachside restaurant by day. The rooftop La Fragata restaurant provides a sensational view of the bay at night. The pool area is rather small and the beach can get crowded, but the restaurants are exceptionally good and the staff couldn't be nicer. Book early—in high season the hotel is often filled with tour groups. *Costera Miguel Alemán 163, 39670, tel. 74/85–55–96 or 800/228–9822. 422 rooms with bath. Facilities: pool, sauna, 2 restaurants, coffee shop, bar, water sports, shops, 5 conference rooms. AE, DC, MC, V.*

$$$
★ **Villa Vera.** This luxury estate, officially the Villa Vera Hotel and Racquet Club, is unequaled in the variety of its accommodations. Some of the villas, which were once private homes, have their own pools. Casa Lisa, the swankest, costs $1,500 a day. Standard rooms, in fashionable pastels and white, are not especially large. By night guests dine at the terraced restaurant, with its stunning view of the bay. For guests who don't have their own cars, transportation is provided by hotel Jeep. *Box 560, Lomas del Mar 35, 39690, tel. 74/84–03–33 or 800/525–4800. 80 rooms with bath. Facilities: pool with swim-up bar, 20 shared and private pools, 3 lighted tennis courts, sauna and massage, beauty salon, restaurant, banquet room. AE, DC, MC, V.*

$$
Autotel Ritz. A good buy for its fairly central location, this hotel attracts bargain hunters and senior citizens. The uncarpeted rooms are simply decorated, but the furniture is chipped and

smudged with paint. Facilities include a restaurant, a decent-size pool with a bar, and room service until 9 PM. Rooms not on the Costera are reasonably quiet. *Ave. Wilfrido Massieu, Box 886, 39670, tel. 74/85–80–23 or 800/448–8355. 100 rooms with bath. Facilities: pool, restaurant, bar. AE, DC, MC, V.*

$$ **Gran Motel Acapulco.** This is a find for its reasonable price and central location. Bare walls and floors and blond-wood furniture give the recently redecorated rooms a monastic appeal. The small pool has a bar, but there is no restaurant. Ask to stay in the old section, where the rooms are larger and quieter and have a partial beach view. *Costera Miguel Alemán 127, 39300, tel. 74/85–59–92. 88 rooms with bath. Facilities: pool, 3 lighted tennis courts, bar, parking. MC, V.*

$$ **Hotel Acapulco Tortuga.** A helpful staff and prime location make the "Turtle Hotel" an appealing choice. It is also one of the few nonbeach hotels to have a garden (handkerchief-size), a beach club (in Puerto Marqués), and a pool where most of the guests hang out. At night the activity shifts to the lobby bar, with the crowd often spilling out onto the street. The downside of this merriment is the noise factor. The best bet is a room facing west on an upper floor. All rooms have blue-green pile rugs and small tables. Breakfast is served in the lobby café; lunch and dinner can be taken in the more formal restaurant. *Costera Miguel Alemán 132, 39300, tel. 74/84–88–89 or 800/832–7491. 252 rooms with bath. Facilities: pool, swim-up bar, lobby bar, 2 restaurants, coffee shop, conference rooms. AE, DC, MC, V.*

$$ **Maralisa Hotel and Beach Club.** Formerly the
★ Villa Vera's sister hotel, this hotel, located on the beach side of the Costera, is now a part of the Howard Johnson chain. The sun deck surrounding two small pools—palm trees and ceramic tiles—is unusual and picturesque. The rooms are light, decorated in whites and pastels. This is a small, friendly place; all rooms have TVs and balconies, and the price is right. *Box 721, Calle Alemania, 39670, tel. 74/85–66–77 or 800/1GO–HOJO. 90 rooms with bath. Facilities: 2 pools, private beach club, water sports, restaurant, bar. AE, DC, MC, V.*

$$ **Ritz.** From its brightly painted exterior, it's
★ clear that the Ritz is serious about vacations.
The lobby is also seriously colorful. Parties are a
hotel specialty; outdoor fiestas are held weekly,
and Friday is Italian night in the Los Carrizos
restaurant. The pink-and-rattan rooms add to
the 1950s beach-party flavor. Accommodations
include mandatory breakfast, tips, and tax. *Box
259, Costera Miguel Alemán and Magallanes,
39580, tel. 74/85–75–44 or 800/527–5919. 252
rooms with bath. Facilities: pool, wading pool,
sauna, water sports, beach clubs, 3 restaurants,
3 bars (including a beach bar), conference
rooms. AE, DC, MC, V.*

Old Acapulco

$$$ **Boca Chica.** This small hotel is in a secluded area
★ on a small peninsula, and its terraced rooms
overlook the bay and Roqueta Island. It's a low-
key place that's a favorite of Mexico City residents in the know. There's a private beach club
with a natural saltwater pool for guests and a
seafood, sushi, and oyster bar. Accommodations
include mandatory breakfast and dinner in high
season. *Caletilla Beach, 39390, tel. 74/83–67–
41. 40 rooms. Facilities: 2 pools. AE, DC, MC,
V.*

$$ **Plaza las Glorias El Mirador.** The old El Mirador
has been taken over by the Plaza las Glorias
chain, which is part of the Sidek conglomerate
responsible for marina and golf developments all
over Mexico. Very Mexican in style—white with
red tiles—the Plaza las Glorias is set high on a
hill with a spectacular view of Acapulco and of
the cliff divers performing at La Quebrada.
*Quebrada 74, 39300, tel. 74/83–11–55 or 800/
342–AMIGO. 143 rooms with bath. Facilities: 3
pools, 2 restaurants (including La Perla restau-
rant-nightclub). AE, DC, MC, V.*

$$ **Suites Alba.** Situated on a quiet hillside in "Acapulco Tradicional," the Alba is a resort-style ho-
tel that offers bargain prices. All rooms and
bungalows are air-conditioned and have a kitch-
enette, private bath, and terrace. There is no
extra charge for up to two children under 12
sharing a room with relatives, which makes it
especially popular with families. Caleta and

Caletilla beaches are within walking distance, but the hotel provides free shuttle service to Caleta during the winter season. *Grand Via Tropical 35, 39390, tel. 74/83–00–73. 250 rooms. Facilities: 3 pools, tennis court, beach club, 3 restaurants, bar, minisupermarket. MC, V.*

$ **Hotel Misión.** Two minutes from the zócalo, this attractive budget hotel is the only colonial hotel in Acapulco. The English-speaking family that runs the Misión lives in a traditional house built in the 19th century. A newer structure housing the guest rooms was added in the 1950s. It surrounds a greenery-rich courtyard with an outdoor dining area. The rooms are small and by no means fancy, with bare cement floors and painted brick walls. But every room has a shower, and sometimes there is even hot water. The best rooms are on the second and third floors; the top-floor room is large but hot in the daytime. *Calle Felipe Valle 12, 39300, tel. 74/82–36–43. 27 rooms, showers only. No credit cards.*

8 The Arts and Nightlife

Acapulco has always been famous for its nightlife, and justifiably so. For many visitors the discos and restaurants are just as important as the sun and the sand. The minute the sun slips over the horizon, the Costera comes alive with people milling around window-shopping, deciding where to dine, and generally biding their time till the disco hour. Obviously you aren't going to find great culture here; theater efforts are few and far between and there is no classical music. But disco-hopping is high art in Acapulco. And for those who care to watch, there are live shows and folk-dance performances. The tour companies listed in the Exploring Acapulco section, above, can organize evening jaunts to most of the dance and music places listed below.

Entertainment

The **Acapulco International Center** (also known as the Convention Center) has a nightly Mexican fiesta featuring mariachi bands, singers, and the "Flying Indians" from Papantla. The show with dinner and drinks costs about $42; entrance to the show alone is $16. Performance with open bar is $23. The buffet dinner starts at 7:30, the performance at 10:15. On Friday, Cantina Night at El Mexicano restaurant in **Las Brisas** hotel, the fiesta starts off with a *tianguis* (marketplace) of handicrafts and ends with a spectacular display of fireworks.

The famous **cliff divers** at La Quebrada (*see* Chapter 3, Exploring Acapulco) give one performance in the afternoon and four performances every night. **Divers de México** organizes sunset champagne cruises that provide a fantastic view of the spectacle from the water. For reservations, call 74/82–13–98, or stop by the office downtown near the *Fiesta* and *Bonanza* yachts. The *Fiesta* (tel. 74/83–18–03) and *Aka Tiki* (74/84–61–40) run nightly cruises with a buffet dinner, open bar (domestic drinks), music, and dancing. Each costs about $45. Or you can take the *Bonanza*'s (tel. 74/83–18–03) sunset cruise with open bar (domestic drinks) for about $20. All boats leave from downtown near the zócalo. Many hotels and shops sell tickets, as do the ticket sellers on the waterfront. At the Colonial, on the Costera, there's a professional **ski show**

Tuesday through Sunday at 9 PM (tel. 74/83–91–07).

Don't forget the nightly entertainment at most hotels. The big resorts have live music to accompany the early evening happy hour, and some feature big-name bands from the United States for less than you would pay at home. Many hotels sponsor theme parties—Italian Night, Beach Party Night, and similar festivities.

Dance

Nina's is a dance hall where the band plays salsa and other Latin rhythms. *On the Costera near CiCi, tel. 74/84–24–00.*

Cats has replaced Antillanos, which replaced the old Cats. In spite of the name change, the ambience remains strictly Antillano's, all palm "trees" and lanterns, with a mostly local crowd. The music is strictly tropical: salsas, cumbias, and mambos. The live groups start playing at 10:30, and at midnight there's a drag show. The $25 cover charge includes local-brand drinks. *Juan de la Cosa 32, tel. 74/84–72–35. Open Tues.–Sun.*

Discos

The legendary Acapulco discos are open 365 days a year from about 10:30 PM until they empty out, often not until 4 or 5 AM. Reservations are advisable for a big group, and late afternoon or after 9 PM are the best times to call. New Year's Eve requires advance planning.

Except for Pyramid Club, Palladium, Fantasy, and Extravaganzza, all the discos are on the Costera and, except for Le Dome, are in three different clusters. They are listed here roughly from east to west:

Pyramid Club, a combination disco and video bar designed to look like a 21st-century Aztec pyramid and equipped with the last word in sound systems, has replaced Tiffany, the posh disco at the Princess Hotel. *Princess Hotel, tel. 74/84–33–95.*

Palladium, inaugurated in December 1993, proves that Acapulco remains the disco capital

of the world. Extravaganzza creator Tony
Rullán has produced another spectacle: a water-
fall that cascades down the hill from the dance-
floor level and makes this place hard to miss. As
at Extravaganzza, the dance floor is nearly sur-
rounded by a huge window, giving dancers a
spectacular view of all Acapulco. *On the Scenic
Highway to Las Brisas, tel. 74/81–03–30.*

Extravaganzza. Vying with Palladium for first
place as Acapulco's most splendiforous disco,
Extravaganzza has the ultimate in light and
sound. It accommodates 700 at a central bar and
in comfortable booths, and a glass wall provides
an unbelievably breathtaking view of Acapulco
Bay. No food is served, but Los Rancheros is
just a few steps away. The music (which is for all
ages) starts at 10:30. *On the Scenic Highway to
Las Brisas, tel. 74/84–71–64.*

Fantasy is one of the most exclusive of all the
discos in Acapulco. If there are any celebrities in
town, they'll be here, rubbing elbows with or
bumping into local fashion designers and artists—since Fantasy is quite snug, to put it nice-
ly. This is one of the only discos where people
really dress up, the men in well-cut pants and
shirts and the women in racy outfits and cocktail
dresses. The crowd is 25–50 and mainly in cou-
ples. Singles gravitate toward the two bars in
the back. A line sometimes forms, so people
come here earlier than they do to other places.
By midnight the dance floor is so packed that
people dance on the wide windowsills that look
out over the bay. At 2 AM there is a fireworks display. A glassed-in elevator provides an interesting overview of the scene and leads upstairs to a
little shop that stocks T-shirts and lingerie. *On
the Scenic Highway, next to Las Brisas, tel. 74/
84–67–27.*

Magic is all black inside and has a fabulous light
show each night after midnight. This is a good-
size place with tables on tiers looking down at
the floor, and it is one of the few discos where on
weekdays you can find a fair number of Mexicans. Any day of the week, this is a good bet to
catch up on the Top 10 from Mexico City, as well
as the American dance hits. The atmosphere is

friendly and laid-back. *Across the Costera from Baby O, tel. 74/84–88–15.*

Baby O and Le Dome (*see below*) are both old favorites. Even midweek, Baby O is packed to the gills. Eschewing the glitz and mirrors of most discos in Acapulco, Baby O resembles a cave in a tropical jungle. The crowd is 18–30 and mostly tourists, although many Mexicans come here, too. In fact, this is one of Acapulco's legendary pickup spots, so feel free to ask someone to dance. When the pandemonium gets to you, retreat to the little hamburger restaurant. *Costera Miguel Alemán 22, tel. 74/84–74–74.*

Hard Rock Cafe, filled with rock memorabilia, is part bar, part restaurant, part dance hall, and part boutique (*see* Chapter 6, Dining).

Le Dome, an Acapulco standby, is still one of the hot spots. Even before the music starts at 11:30, there is already a small crowd at the door, and in spite of the capacity of 800, this club is always full. Le Dome doesn't look very different from other clubs on the Costera—it has the usual black wall and mirror mix, although it does have a larger video screen than most. Le Dome is the only club in Acapulco, if not in the world, where you can play basketball—yes, basketball—every Wednesday. Winners get a bottle of tequila. *Costera Miguel Alemán 402, next door to Fiorucci, tel. 74/84–11–90.*

Discobeach is Acapulco's only alfresco disco and its most informal one. The under-30 crowd sometimes even turns up in shorts. The waiters are young and friendly, and every night they dress to a different theme. One night they're all in togas carrying bunches of grapes, the next they're in pajamas. Every Wednesday, ladies' night, all the women receive flowers. The coco loco is the house special. *On Condesa Beach, tel. 74/84–70–64.*

News is enormous, with seating for 1,200 people in love seats and booths. There are different theme parties and competitions nightly—bikini contests on Tuesday and Carnival Night (with lambada and limbo contests and a Brazilian-style show) on Thursday. Winners walk off with a bottle of champagne or dinner for two; occasionally the prize has been a trip to Hawaii. From 10:30 (opening time) to 11:30, the music is slow and romantic; then the disco music and the light show begin, and they go on till dawn. *Costera Miguel Alemán, across from the Hyatt Regency, tel. 74/84–59–02.*

9 Excursions from Acapulco

Taxco, the Silver City

It's a picture-postcard look—Mexico in its Sunday best: white stucco buildings nuzzling cobblestoned streets, red-tiled roofs and geranium-filled window boxes bright in the sun. Taxco (pronounced *TAHSS-co*), a colonial treasure that the Mexican government declared a national monument in 1928, tumbles onto the hills of the Sierra Madre in the state of Guerrero. Its silver mines have drawn people here for centuries. Now its charm, mild temperatures, sunshine, and flowers make Taxco a popular tourist destination.

Hernán Cortés discovered Taxco's mines in 1522. The silver rush lasted until the next century, when excitement tapered off. Then in the 1700s a Frenchman, who Mexicanized his name to José de la Borda, discovered a rich lode that revitalized the town's silver industry and made him exceedingly wealthy. After Borda, however, Taxco's importance faded, until the 1930s and the arrival of William G. Spratling, a writer-architect from New Orleans. Enchanted by Taxco and convinced of its potential as a silver center, Spratling set up an apprentice shop, where his artistic talent and his fascination with pre-Columbian design combined to produce silver jewelry and other artifacts that soon earned Taxco its worldwide reputation as the Silver City. Spratling's inspiration lives on in his students and their descendants, many of whom are the city's current silversmiths.

Getting There

There are several ways to travel to Taxco from Acapulco, and all involve ground transport.

By Car It takes about 3 hours to make the drive from Acapulco to Taxco, using the new—and very expensive—toll road. It is common practice to hire a chauffeured car or a taxi. Check with your hotel for references and prices.

By Bus First-class **Estrella de Oro** buses leave Acapulco several times a day from the Terminal Central de Autobuses de Primera Clase (Av. Cuauhtémoc 1490, tel. 74/85–87–05). The cost for the approximately four-hour ride is about $15 one way for deluxe service. The Taxco terminal is at Avenida John F. Kennedy 126 (tel. 762/2–06–48). First-class **Flecha Roja** buses depart Acapulco several times a day from the Terminal de Autobuses (Ejido 47, tel. 74/83–12–51). The one-way ticket is about $12 for first-class service. The Taxco terminal for this line is at Avenida John F. Kennedy 104 (tel. 762/2–01–31).

Getting Around

Unless you're used to byways, alleys, and tiny streets, maneuvering anything bigger than your two feet through Taxco will be difficult. Fortunately, almost everything of interest is within walking distance of the zócalo. Minibuses travel along preset routes and charge only a few cents, and Volkswagen "bugs" provide inexpensive (average $2) taxi transportation. Remember that Taxco's altitude is 5,800 feet. Wear sensible shoes for negotiating the hilly streets, and if you have come from sea level, take it easy on your first day.

Exploring

Numbers in the margin correspond to points of interest on the Taxco Exploring map.

❶
❷ Begin at the **zócalo,** properly called **Plaza Borda,** heading first into the **Church of San Sebastián and Santa Prisca,** which dominates the main square. Usually just called Santa Prisca, it was built by French silver magnate José de la Borda in thanks to the Almighty for his having literally stumbled upon a rich silver vein. The style of the church—sort of Spanish Baroque meets Rococo—is known as Churrigueresque, and its pink exterior is a stunning surprise.

❸ Just a block from the zócalo, behind Santa Prisca, is the **Spratling Museum,** formerly the home of William G. Spratling (*see* Introduction, *above*). This wonderful little museum explains the working of colonial mines and displays Spratling's collection of pre-Columbian artifacts. *Porfirio Delgado and El Arco. Small entrance fee. Open Tues.–Sat. 10–5.*

Taxco Exploring

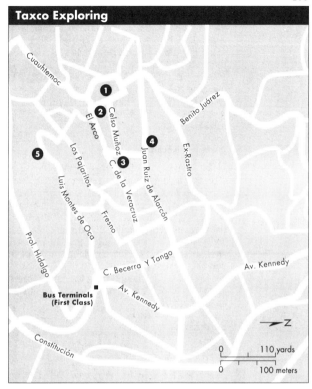

Casa
Humboldt, **4**

Municipal
Maarket, **5**

Plaza Borda
(Zócalo), **1**

Santa Prisca, **2**

Spratling
Museum, **3**

4 **Casa Humboldt,** a block away, was named for the German adventurer Alexander von Humboldt, who stayed here in 1803. The Moorish-style 18th-century house has a finely detailed facade. It now houses a museum of colonial art. *Calle Juan Ruíz Alarcón 6. No entrance fee. Open Fri.–Sat.*

5 Down the hill from Santa Prisca is the **Municipal Market,** which is worth a visit, especially early on Saturday or Sunday morning.

Time Out Around the plaza are several *neverías* where you can treat yourself to an ice cream in a delicious fruit flavor, such as coconut. **Bar Paco's,** directly across the street from Santa Prisca, is a Taxco institution; its terrace is the perfect vantage point for watching the comings and goings on the zócalo while sipping a margarita or a beer.

Off the Beaten Track

About 15 minutes northeast of Taxco are the Caves of Cacahuamilpa (Grutas de Cacahuamilpa). The largest caverns in Mexico, these 15 large chambers comprise 12 kilometers (8 miles) of geological formation. Only some caves are illuminated. A guide can be hired at the entrance to the caves.

Shopping

Silver Most of the people who visit Taxco come with silver in mind. Three types are available: sterling, which is always stamped .925 (925 parts in 1,000) and is the most expensive; plated silver; and the inexpensive *alpaca*, which is also known as German silver or nickel silver. Sterling pieces are usually priced by weight according to world silver prices, and of course fine workmanship will add to the cost. Work is also done with semiprecious stones; you'll find garnets, topazes, amethysts, and opals. If you plan to buy, check prices before leaving home. When comparison shopping in the more than 200 silver shops in Taxco, you will see that many carry almost identical merchandise, although a few are noted for their creativity. Among them:

Elena de los Ballesteros (Celso Muñoz 4) is a very elegant shop with work of outstanding design.
Galería de Arte Andrés (Av. John F. Kennedy 28) has unique designs created by the personable Andrés Mejía.
Los Castillo (Plazuela Bernal 10) is the most famous and decidedly one of the most exciting silver shops; it's known for innovative design and for combining silver with ceramics and such other metals as copper and brass. The artisans are disciples of Spratling.
Pineda's Taxco (Plaza Borda) has fine designs and fine workmanship.
Spratling Ranch (south of town on Highway 95) is where the heirs of William Spratling turn out designs using his original molds.

Local Wares Lacquered gourds and boxes from the town of Olinalá, masks, bowls, straw baskets, bark paintings, and many other handcrafted items native to the state of Guerrero are available from strolling vendors and are displayed on the cobblestones at "sidewalk boutiques." **Arnoldo's** (Palma 1) has an interesting collection of ceremonial masks. **Gracias a Dios** (Bernal 3) carries women's clothing, with brightly colored ribbons and appliqués, designed by Tachi Castillo, as well as a less original selection of crafts. **La Calleja** (Calle Arco 5, 2nd floor) offers a wide and well-chosen selection of native arts and handicrafts.

Sunday is market day, which means that artisans from surrounding villages descend on the town, as do visitors from Mexico City. It can get crowded, but if you find a seat on a bench in Plaza Borda, you're set to watch the show and peruse the merchandise that will inevitably be brought to you.

Sports and Fitness

You can play golf or tennis, swim, and ride horses at various hotels around Taxco. Call to see if the facilities are open to nonguests. Bullfights are occasionally held in the small town of Acmixtla, 6 kilometers (3.75 miles) from Taxco. Ask at your hotel about the schedule.

Dining

Gastronomes can find everything from tagliatelle to iguana in Taxco restaurants, and meals are much less expensive than in Acapulco. Highly recommended restaurants are indicated by a star ★.

Category	Cost*
$$$$	over $20
$$$	$15–$20
$$	$8–$15
$	under $8

per person excluding drinks, service, and sales tax (10%)

★ **La Ventana de Taxco.** The Italian recipes inherited from the former manager, Mario Cavagna, coupled with Mexican specialties and a fantastic view, make this the town's finest restaurant and one of the best in all Mexico. *Hacienda del Solar Hotel, Hwy. 95, south of town, tel. 762/2–05–87. Reservations required on weekends. Dress: casual. MC, V. $$$$*

Pagaduría del Rey. In the Posada Don Carlos, south of town via Avenida John F. Kennedy, this restaurant has a long-standing reputation for Continental fare served in comfortable surroundings. *Calle H. Colegio Militar 8 (Colonia Cerro de la Bermeja), tel. 762/2–34–67. Reservations not necessary. Dress: casual. No lunch. MC, V. $$$$*

Toni's. Prime rib and lobster are the specialties. There's also a great view and a romantic setting. *Monte Taxco Hotel, tel. 762/2–13–00. Reservations required. Dress: casual. AE, DC, MC, V. $$$$*

Cielito Lindo. This charming restaurant features a Mexican-international menu. Give the Mexican specialties a try—for example, *pollo en pipián verde*, a chicken simmered in a mild, pumpkinseed-based sauce. *Plaza Borda, tel. 762/2–06–03. No reservations. Dress: casual. MC, V. $$$*

★ **La Taberna.** This is another successful venture of the proprietors of Bora Bora, Taxco's popular pizza place. The menu is varied, with the likes of pastas, beef Stroganoff, and crepes to choose from. *Benito Juárez 8, tel. 762/2–52–26. Reservations advised. Dress: casual. MC, V. $$$*

★ **Bora Bora.** Exceptionally good pizza is what's on the menu here. *Callejón de las Delícias 4, behind Paco's Bar, tel. 762/2–17–21. No reservations. Dress: casual. MC, V. $$*

Piccolo Mondo. More casual than its neighbor, Toni's, this place serves pizza baked in a wood-burning brick oven and meats and chicken charcoal-broiled at your table. *Monte Taxco Hotel, tel. 762/2–13–00. Reservations advised. Dress: casual. AE, DC, MC, V. Closed Mon.–Thurs. $$*

Señor Costilla. That's right. This translates as Mr. Ribs, and the whimsical name says it all. The Taxco outpost of the zany Anderson chain serves ribs and chops in a restaurant with great balcony seating. *Plaza Borda, tel. 762/2–32–15. Reservations advised. Dress: casual. MC, V. $$*

La Hacienda. In the Hotel Agua Escondida, this charming restaurant serves Mexican and international specialties. The best buy: the daily fixed-price *comida corrida. Guillermo Spratling 4, tel. 762/2–06–63. No reservations. Dress: casual. MC, V. $*

Lodging

Whether your stay in Taxco is a one-night stopover or a few days' respite from the madness of Acapulco, there are several categories of hotel to choose from within Taxco's two types: the small inns nestled on the hills skirting the zócalo and the larger, more modern hotels on the outskirts of town. Highly recommended lodgings are indicated by a star ★ .

Category	Cost*
$$$$	over $90
$$$	$60–$90

$$	$25–$60
$	under $25

All prices are for standard double room, exluding 10% sales (called IVA) tax.

Monte Taxco. A colonial style predominates at this hotel, which has a knockout view and two restaurants, a disco, and nightly entertainment. *Box 84, Lomas de Taxco, 40200, tel. 762/ 2–13–00. 188 rooms, suites, and villas with bath. Facilities: 3 tennis courts, 9-hole golf course, horseback riding, 3 restaurants, disco. AE, DC, MC, V. $$$$*

★ **Hacienda del Solar.** This intimate and elegant small resort (off Hwy. 95 south of town) has well-appointed rooms. Its restaurant is the top-notch La Ventana de Taxco (*see above*). *Box 96, 40200, tel. 762/2–03–23. 22 rooms with bath. Facilities: tennis court, pool, restaurant. MC, V. $$$*

★ **Posada de la Misión.** Laid out like a village, this hotel is close to town and has dining-room murals by the noted Mexican artist Juan O'Gorman. *Box 88, Cerro de la Misión 84, 40230, tel. 762/2–00–63. 150 rooms with bath. Facilities: pool, tennis court. AE, DC, MC, V. $$$*

Rancho Taxco-Victoria. This in-town hotel, in two buildings connected by a bridge over the road, is under the same management as the De la Borda (*see below*) and suffers from the same neglect. It has its rooms done in classic Mexican decor. There's also the requisite splendid view. *Box 83, Carlos J. Nibbi 5, 40200, tel. 762/2–02– 10. 64 rooms with bath. Facilities: 2 pools, restaurant, bar. AE, MC, V. $$$*

Agua Escondida. A favorite with some regular visitors to Taxco, this small hotel has simple rooms decorated with Mexican-style furnishings. *Guillermo Spratling 4, 40200, tel. 762/2– 07–26. 50 rooms with bath. Facilities: pool, La Hacienda restaurant. MC, V. $$*

De la Borda. Long a Taxco favorite, but getting very run-down now, this hotel has rooms overlooking town from a hillside perch. There's a restaurant with occasional entertainment, and many bus tours en route from Mexico City to Acapulco stay here overnight. *Box 6, Cerro del*

Pedregal 2, 40200, tel. 762/2–00–25. 95 rooms with bath. Facilities: pool, restaurant. MC, V. $$

Loma Linda. This is a basic motel on the highway just east of town. *Av. John F. Kennedy 52, 40200, tel. 762/2–02–06. 55 units. Facilities: pool, restaurant, bar. AE, MC, V. $$*

Los Arcos. An in-town inn, Los Arcos offers basic accommodations around a pleasant patio. *Calle Juan Ruíz de Alarcón, 40200, tel. 762/2–18–36. 25 rooms with bath. MC, V. $$*

Posada de los Castillo. This inn in town is straightforward, clean, and good for the price. *Juan Ruíz de Alarcón 7, 40200, tel. 762/2–13–96. 15 rooms. Facilities: restaurant, bar. DC, MC, V. $$*

Santa Prisca. The patio with fountains is a plus at this colonial-style hotel. *Cena Obscuras 1, 40200, tel. 762/2–00–80. 40 rooms. Facilities: restaurant, bar. AE, MC, V. $$*

The Arts and Nightlife

The Arts Taxco has no abundance of cultural events, but it's noted for its festivals, which are an integral part of the town's character. These fiestas provide an opportunity to honor almost every saint in heaven with music, dancing, marvelous fireworks, and lots of fun. The people of Taxco demonstrate their pyrotechnical skills with set pieces—wondrous blazing "castles" made of bamboo. (Note: Expect high occupancy at local hotels and inns during fiestas.)

January 18, the feast of Santa Prisca and San Sebastián, the town's patron saints, is celebrated with music and fireworks.

Holy Week, from Palm Sunday to Easter Sunday, brings processions and events that blend Christian and Indian traditions, the dramas involving hundreds of participants, images of Christ, and, for one particular procession, black-hooded penitents. Most events are centered on Plaza Borda and the Santa Prisca Church.

September 29, Saint Michael's Day (Día de San Miguel), is celebrated with regional dances and pilgrimages to the Chapel of Saint Michael the Archangel.

In **early November,** on the Monday following the Day of the Dead celebrations on November 1 and 2, the entire town takes off to a nearby hill for the Fiesta de los Jumiles. The *jumil* is a crawling insect that is said to taste strongly of iodine and is considered a great delicacy. Purists eat them alive, but others prefer them stewed, fried, or combined with chili in a hot sauce.

In **late November or early December,** the National Silver Fair (Feria Nacional de la Plata) draws hundreds of artisans from around the world for a variety of displays, concerts, exhibitions, and contests held around the city.

Nightlife Travelers should satisfy their appetite for fun after dark in Acapulco. Although Taxco has one or two discos, a couple of piano bars, and some entertainment, the range is limited.

Still, you might enjoy spending an evening perched on a chair on a balcony or in one of the cafés surrounding the Plaza Borda. Two traditional favorites are the **Bar Paco** and **Bertha's,** where a tequila, lime, and club-soda concoction called a Bertha is the house specialty.

Or immerse yourself in the thick of things, especially on Sunday evening, by settling in on a wrought-iron bench on the zócalo to watch children, lovers, and fellow people-watchers.

Most of Taxco's nighttime activity is at the Monte Taxco hotel, either at the **Windows** discotheque or at **Tony Reyes's,** where the price of the show includes a performance of the Papantla fliers, dancing, drinks, and transportation. On Saturday nights there's a buffet, a terrific fireworks display (Taxco is Mexico's fireworks capital), and a show put on by the hotel's employees.

Some of the best restaurants, including La Ventana de Taxco, have music.

Ixtapa and Zihuatanejo

In Ixtapa/Zihuatanejo, 3½ hours by car (250 kilometers/150 miles) up the coast from Acapulco, you can enjoy two distinct lifestyles for the price of one—double value for your money.

Ixtapa/Zihuatanejo is a complete change of pace from hectic Acapulco. The water is comfortably warm for swimming, and the waves are gentle. The temperature averages 78° year-round. During the mid-December–Easter high season, the weather is sunny and dry, and in the June–October rainy season the short, heavy showers usually fall at night.

Ixtapa (pronounced *eeks-TAH-pa*), where most Americans stay—probably because they can't pronounce Zihuatanejo (*see-wha-tah-NAY-ho*)—is big, modern, and young, established in 1976. Exclusively a vacation resort, it was invented and planned, as was Cancún, by Fonatur, Mexico's National Fund for Tourism Development. Large world-class hotels cluster in the Hotel Zone around Palmar Bay, where conditions are ideal for swimming and water sports, and just across the street are a couple of football fields' worth of shopping malls. The hotels are well spaced; there's always plenty of room on the beach, which is lighted for strolling at night; and the pace is leisurely.

Zihuatanejo, which means "land of women" in Purepecha, the language of the Tarascan Indians, lies 7 kilometers (3 miles) to the southeast. According to legend, Caltzontzin, a Tarascan king, chose this bay as his royal retreat and enclosed it with a long protective breakwater, which is known today as Las Gatas. Zihuatanejo is an old fishing village that has managed to retain its charm; but it's also the area's municipal center, and its *malecón* (waterfront) and brick streets are lined with hotels, restaurants, and boutiques.

Getting There

By Plane   You can fly to Ixtapa on **Mexicana Airlines** from San Francisco and Los Angeles via Guadalajara, and from Chicago via Mexico City. **Delta** flies to Ixtapa nonstop from Los Angeles. Both **Mexicana** and **Aeromexico** have daily nonstop service from Mexico City and most other major cities in Mexico, but there is no direct air service from Acapulco. **Aeromar** (tel. 5/627–0205 in Mexico City, 74/84–07–69 in Acapulco, 743/

42683 in Ixtapa) offers daily nonstop service between Mexico City and Ixtapa.

By Car The trip from Acapulco is a 3½-hour drive over a good road that passes through small towns and coconut groves and has some quite spectacular ocean views for the last third of the way. At three inspection stops, soldiers checking for drugs and arms generally only look into the car and wave you on.

By Bus **Estrella de Oro** and **Flecha Roja** offer deluxe service (which means that the air-conditioning and toilets are likely to be functioning) between Acapulco and Zihuatanejo. The trip takes about four hours and costs $13. You must reserve and pick up your ticket one day in advance and get to the terminal at least a half hour before departure. Estrella de Oro buses leave from the Terminal Central de Autobuses de Primera Clase (Av. Cuauhtémoc 1490, tel. 74/85–87–05). The Flecha Roja buses leave from the Terminal de Autobuses (Ejido 47, tel. 74/83–12–51).

Escorted Tours

Most Acapulco-based travel agencies can set up one-day tours to Ixtapa/Zihuatanejo for about $50–$150, including guide, transportation (car, minibus, or bus), and lunch. If your hotel travel desk can't make these arrangements for you, contact **Turismo Caleta** (Calle Andrea Dória 2, tel. 74/86–28–31), **Fantasy Tours** (Costera Miguel Alemán 50, tel. 74/84–25–28), or **Turismo Las Hamacas** (Las Hamacas hotel, tel. 74/83–00–34).

For another perspective, take a 6½-hour cruise for $45 on **Brisas del Mar's** 12-passenger trimaran *Tri-Star* (tel. 753/4–27–48) or on the *Las Brisas*, operated by **Sailboats of the Sun** (tel. 753/4–20–91). Both set sail from the Puerto Mío marina in Zihuatanejo and include open bar (domestic drinks), live music, dancing, and a fresh-fish lunch at Ixtapa Island. Both the *Tri-Star* and *Las Brisas* have two-hour sunset cruises of Zihuatanejo Bay. On Thursday and Saturday nights, the *Tri-Star* operates "The Night Flight"; $40 includes live music, snacks, open bar, and dancing.

Getting Around

Unless you plan to travel great distances or visit remote beaches, taxis and buses are by far the best way to get around. Rental cars (automatic shift and air-conditioning) cost about $100 per day; Jeeps about $75.

By Taxi Taxis are plentiful, and fares are reasonable. The average fare from the Ixtapa Hotel Zone to Zihuatanejo, Playa La Ropa, or Playa Quieta is about $6.50. There's no problem getting cabs, and there are taxi stands in front of most hotels.

By Bus The buses that operate between the hotels and from the Hotel Zone to downtown Zihuatanejo run approximately every 20 minutes and charge about 20¢.

By Motor Scooter Scooters can be rented at **Hola Renta Motos** (in the Los Patios shopping center, across from the Dorado Pacífico hotel, no phone) for $10–$15 an hour.

By Pedicab Pedicabs (*cucarachas*) decorated with balloons can be rented in the shopping mall across the street from the Dorado Pacífico hotel for $10 per hour. Bikes cost $2 per hour. The rental tent is open daily 9–8.

By Car Rental-car offices in Zihuatanejo: **Budget** at the Dorado Pacífico hotel (tel. 753/3–20–25), **Dollar** at the Hotel Krystal (tel. 753/3–03–33, ext. 1110), and **Hertz** (Calle Nicolás Bravo 10, tel. 753/4–30–50 or 753/4–22–55). In Ixtapa: **Avis's** only office is in the airport (tel. 753/4–22–48), and the other companies have branches there. Jeeps can be rented at the airport from **Dollar** (tel. 753/4–23–14).

Exploring

No matter where you go in Ixtapa/Zihuatanejo, you get the fresh-air, great-outdoors feeling of a place in the making, with plenty of room to spare.

Zihuatanejo is a tropical charmer. The seaside promenade overlooks the town dock and cruise-ship pier; tiny bars and restaurants invite you to linger longer. From town the road soars up a hill that has a handful of restaurants and hotels perched on breezy spots overlooking the bay.

Another sprinkling of hotels surround pancake-flat **Madera Beach. La Ropa,** farther along, is Zihuatanejo's most popular beach and the location of one of Mexico's best small hotels, Villa del Sol. **Las Gatas** beach, beyond, lined with dive shops and tiny restaurants, is also popular but is accessible only by water.

At the opposite end of the area, about five minutes beyond the Ixtapa Hotel Zone, is pretty **Playa Quieta,** a small beach used by Club Med. From here you can take a boat ride to **Isla Ixtapa,** about $2, and spend a wonderful day in the sun far from other people. Once the boat lands, take the path to the other side of the island for better sunning and swimming.

Shopping

At last count there were seven shopping malls in Ixtapa. La Puerta, the first one built, is now flanked by terra-cotta-colored Ixpamar, colonial-style Los Patios, and bright white Las Fuentes. The ubiquitous **Aca Joe** and **Polo Ralph Lauren** are in Las Fuentes, as is **Africán,** which carries 100%-cotton safari-style clothing for men and women. **El Baul,** with handicrafts from the state of Guerrero, is in La Puerta; **Chiquita Banana,** a good source of decorative items for your house, and **La Fuente,** which sells clothes with native-inspired designs, are in Los Patios. **El Huizteco,** which sells some of the best folk art in the state, is in Ixpamar. Don't let the modern facades and sparkling decor fool you: Most prices are within everyone's range. There is sometimes free live entertainment on the patio at Ixpamar.

Downtown Zihuatanejo has a municipal minimarket and a host of tiny stores. You must go inside to discover bargains in souvenirs and decorations, T-shirts, and embroidered dresses. On Calle Vicente Guerrero is one of the best handicrafts shops in all of Mexico—**Coco Cabaña,** which is owned by the same people who run Coconuts restaurant. **Los Almendros,** at Calles Guerrero and Alvarez, has an especially good selection of handpainted ceramics from Oaxaca, and at **La Zapoteca,** on the waterfront, you'll find hand-loomed woolen rugs, wall hangings, and hammocks. On Calle Juan N. Alvarez, Indians sell baskets and other handmade wares that they bring from the surrounding areas.

Sports and Fitness

Although several hotels have tennis courts and there are two beautiful championship golf courses in Ixtapa, most of the outdoor activities in Ixtapa/Zihuatanejo center on the water. At the **water-sports center** in front of Villa del Sol on La Ropa you can arrange for waterskiing, snorkeling, diving, and windsurfing.

Deep-sea Fishing Boats with captain and crew can be hired at the **Cooperativa de Lanchas de Recreo and Pesca Deportiva** (Av. Ruíz Cortines 40 at the Zihuatanejo pier; tel. 753/4-20-56) or through **Turismo Caleta** (La Puerta shopping center in Ixtapa, tel. 753/3-04-44). The cost is $80 to $100 for a boat with two lines and up to $250 for a boat with four to six lines.

Golf and Tennis The **Ixtapa Golf Club** (tel. 753/3-11-63) is open to the public. The greens fee is $50; tennis costs $8 an hour in the daytime, $10 at night. Caddies cost $17 a round and carts go for $33. A second 18-hole golf course is located at Marina Ixtapa but is not open to the public. Most of the hotels in Ixtapa and a few in Zihuatanejo have tennis courts; nonguests can usually play for a fee.

Horseback Riding You can rent horses at La Manzanilla Ranch, near Playa La Ropa, and at Playa Linda.

Parasailing You can try this scary-looking sport on the beach in the Ixtapa Hotel Zone. A 10-minute ride will cost about $15.

Sailing Hobie Cats and larger sailboats are available for rent at La Ropa Beach and Marina Ixtapa for $20–$60 per hour.

Scuba Diving The **Zihuatanejo Scuba Center,** at Calle Cuauhtémoc 3 (tel. 753/4-21-47), is operated by marine biologist Juan Barnard Avila. The staff, which includes some expatriate Americans, is enthusiastic and knowledgeable. The single-tank dive costs $45 ($40 if you have your own gear); the double-tank dive costs $70 ($60 without equipment) and includes two separate dives and lunch.

Windsurfing This popular activity can be arranged at Las Gatas and La Ropa beaches for about $20 per hour—$30 per hour with lessons.

Dining

Meals are generally less expensive in downtown Zihuatanejo than in Ixtapa or in the restaurants up in the hills, and even the most expensive ones will cost considerably less than those in Acapulco. The restaurants will fall at the lower end of our price categories, verging on the category below, and casual dress is acceptable everywhere. Highly recommended restaurants are indicated by a star ★.

Category	Cost*
$$$$	over $35
$$$	$25–$35
$$	$15–$25
$	under $15

per person excluding drinks, service, and sales tax (10%)

Ixtapa **Bogart's.** This restaurant is romantic and elegant, with Moorish-Arabic decor and an international menu. The *Crepas Persas* (Persian crepes) filled with cheese are topped with sour cream and caviar. Or try *Suprema Casablanca*: chicken breasts stuffed with lobster then breaded and fried. *Hotel Krystal, Playa Palmar, tel. 753/3–03–33. Reservations required. No shorts or T-shirts. AE, DC, MC, V. $$$*

El Faro. El Faro sits atop a hill next to the funicular that goes up to the Club Pacífica complex. It has an extensive menu that includes *camarones en salsa de albahaca* (shrimp in a basil sauce). Other draws are piano music and a spectacular view. *Playa Vista Hermosa, tel. 753/3–10–27. Reservations advised. Dress: casual. AE, MC, V. $$$*

El Sombrero. This popular place serves Mexican food, seafood, and international dishes. The potpourri Mexicana, with chicken in mole sauce, an enchilada, and a spicy sausage, is a good introduction to real Mexican cookery. *Los Patios*

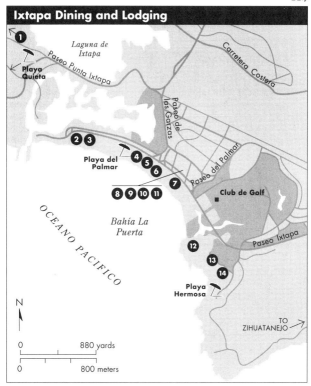

Ixtapa Dining and Lodging

Dining

Bogart's, **4**
Café Onyx, **9**
Carlos 'n Charlie's, **2**
Da Baffone, **8**
El Faro, **12**
El Sombrero, **10**
Las Esferas, **13**
Nueva Zelanda, **11**
Villa de la Selva, **14**

Lodging

Casa de la Tortuga, **1**
Dorado Pacífico, **6**
Krystal Ixtapa, **5**
Posada Real, **1**
Presidente, **7**
Westin Ixtapa, **13**

shopping center, tel. 753/3–04–39. Reservations advised. Dress: casual. MC, V. Closed Sun. $$$

★ **Las Esferas.** This place in the Westin Ixtapa is a complex of two restaurants and a bar. **Portofino** specializes in Italian cuisine and is decorated with multicolored pastas and scenes of Italy. In **El Mexicano** the specialties are naturally Mexican, as is the decor—bright pink tablecloths, Puebla jugs, a huge tree of life, antique wood carvings, and blown glass. *Playa Vista Hermosa, tel. 753/3–21–21, ext. 3444. Reservations necessary at Portofino, advised at El Mexicano. No shorts or T-shirts. AE, DC, MC, V. $$$*

Villa de la Selva. Just past the Westin Ixtapa, this restaurant has tables set up on multilevel terraces under the stars. Excellent international dishes, grilled steaks, and seafood are served in a romantic setting, and special lighting after dark illuminates the sea and the rocks below. *Paseo de la Roca, tel. 753/3–03–62. Reservations advised. Dress: casual. AE, MC, V. No lunch. $$$*

Carlos 'n' Charlie's. Hidden away at the end of the beach, this outpost of the famous Anderson's chain serves pork, seafood, and chicken in a Polynesian setting almost on the sand. It has a minizoo, too. *Next to Posada Real Hotel, tel. 753/3–00–35. No reservations. Dress: casual. AE, DC, MC, V. $$*

Da Baffone. The atmosphere is easy and informal at this well-run Italian restaurant with two dining areas; you can choose the air-conditioned dining room or the open-air porch. Try the spaghetti *siubeco*, prepared with cream, peppers, shrimp, and wine. *La Puerta shopping mall, tel. 753/3–11–22. Reservations advised. Dress: casual. AE, MC, V. $$*

Café Onyx. Mexican and international dishes are served under an awning at this alfresco eatery. *Across from the Holiday Inn, in the Galerías shopping mall, tel. 753/3–03–46. No reservations. Dress: casual. MC, V. $*

★ **Nueva Zelanda.** This is a fast-moving cafeteria with good food that you order by numbers. Chicken enchiladas with green sauce, *sincronizadas* (flour tortillas filled with ham and cheese), and the *licuados* (milk shakes with fresh fruit) are all tasty. Families with young children gather here, and there is usually a line on weekends. Dinner for two can cost less than $10. *Behind the bandstand, no phone. No reservations. No credit cards. $*

Zihuatanejo **Coconuts.** Excellent seafood and salads are served in elegant surroundings. *Calle Agustín Ramírez 1, tel. 753/4–25–18. Reservations required. Dress: casual. AE, MC, V. Closed Sept.–Oct. $$$*

★ **La Casa Que Canta.** Sheltered under a thatched roof and set on a cliff overlooking Zihuatanejo Bay, this appealing restaurant was created by Ercolino Crugnale, executive chef at the Stouffer Stanford Court in San Francisco. His international menu includes Continental, Mexican, and seafood selections. Breads and cakes are baked each day on the premises. *La Casa Que Canta hotel, Camino Escénico a Playa La Ropa, tel. 753/4–27–22. Dinner only for nonguests. No children under 16. Reservations required. Dress: casual. AE, DC, MC, V. $$$*

★ **Villa del Sol.** This restaurant, in the hotel that bears the same name, has earned a worldwide reputation for excellent quality and service. The international menu is prepared by Swiss, German, and Mexican chefs. *Hotel Villa del Sol, Playa La Ropa, tel. 753/4–22–39. Dinner reservations advised. Dress: casual. No credit cards. $$$*

Casa Elvira. Elvira Reyes, the owner, claims that this is the oldest restaurant in town—it's been around since 1956. It's quaint and clean, decorated with Talavera tiles and handicrafts from Pátzcuaro, and the prices are reasonable. There's a fairly large selection of fish and seafood, including an excellent *parrillada de mariscos* (seafood grill), as well as such traditional Mexican dishes as poblano peppers stuffed with cheese and *puntas de filete albañil* (a kind of stew). *Paseo del Pescador 16, tel. 753/4–20–61. MC, V. $$*

Garrabos. This delightful restaurant specializes in seafood and Mexican cuisine. Try the seafood brochettes. *Calle Juan N. Alvarez 52, near the church and museum, tel. 753/4–29–77. Reservations advised. Dress: casual. MC, V. $$*

★ **Tabaga.** *Pescado Yugoslavia* (fillet of fish prepared with cheese, potatoes, and vegetables) is just one of the tasty seafood dishes served in this

Zihuatanejo Dining and Lodging

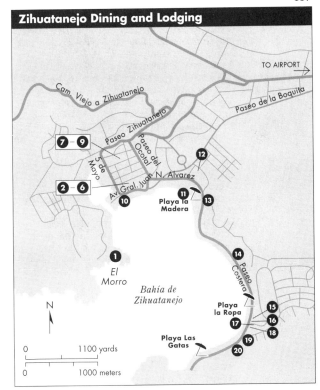

TO AIRPORT

Cam. Viejo a Zihuatanejo

Paseo de la Boquita

Paseo Zihuatanejo

Paseo del Ocotal

7 – 9

5 de Mayo

2 – 6

Av. Gral. Juan N. Álvarez

10

12

11

13

Playa la Madera

1

El Morro

14

Paseo Costera

Bahía de Zihuatanejo

N

15

Playa la Ropa

17

16

18

19

20

Playa Las Gatas

| 0 | 1100 yards |
| 0 | 1000 meters |

Dining
Casa Elvira, **7**
Coconuts, **9**
Garrabos, **2**
La Bocana, **3**
La Casa Que Canta, **17**
La Gaviota, **16**
La Perla, **20**

La Sirena Gorda, **4**
Nueva Zelanda, **8**
Puntarenas, **5**
Tabaga, **10**
Villa del Sol, **20**

Lodging
Avila, **6**
Bungalows Pacíficos, **11**
Catalina-Sotovento, **14**
Fiesta Mexicana, **15**
Irma, **13**

La Csa Que Canta, **17**
Puerto Mío, **1**
Villa del Sol, **20**
Villas las Urracas, **19**
Villas Miramar, **12**

quaint, recently renovated place across from the Aeromexico office. *Calle Juan N. Alvarez and Cinco de Mayo, tel. 753/4–26–37. No reservations. Dress: casual. MC, V. $$*

La Bocana. This restaurant is a favorite with locals as well as visitors. The service is good and the seafood is a treat. You can eat three meals a day here. Musicians sometimes stroll through. *Calle Juan N. Alvarez 13, tel. 753/4–35–45. Dress: casual. MC, V. $*

La Gaviota. At this mini-beach club you can spend an afternoon swimming and sunning after having a seafood lunch. Lots of locals like this one, and the bar is pleasant. Ask the taxi driver to come back for you around 4 PM. *On Playa La Ropa, tel. 753/4–38–16. No reservations. Dress: casual. MC, V. $*

La Perla. At Doña Raquel's popular seaside restaurant and video sports bar, the hands-down favorite is *Filete La Perla*, a fish fillet baked in aluminum foil with cheese, garlic, onion, and tomato. *Playa La Ropa, tel. 753/4–27–00. Dress: casual. MC, V. $*

La Sirena Gorda. The specialty here is seafood tacos (try the shrimp-and-bacon combo); meals are served in rustic yet pleasant surroundings. *Paseo del Pescador 20-A, tel. 753/4–26–87. Dress: casual. MC, V. Open Thurs.–Tues. 7 AM–10 PM. $*

★ **Nueva Zelanda.** From breakfast through dinner everybody drops in to this little coffee shop–style eatery, which serves *tortas* (Mexican sandwiches on crusty rolls), tacos, and enchiladas. *Calle Cuauhtémoc 23, no phone. No reservations. Dress: casual. No credit cards. $*

Puntarenas. This plain place serves Mexican food and great breakfasts. It's a favorite with those in the know and there's often a line, but it's worth the wait. *Across the bridge at the end of Calle Juan N. Alvarez, no phone. No reservations. Dress: casual. No credit cards. Open only in high season. $*

Lodging

Ixtapa/Zihuatanejo hotel rates vary widely, and after Easter they drop 30%–40% and sometimes more. Most of the budget accommodations are in Zihuatanejo, where the best hotels are on or overlooking La Madera or La Ropa Beach and the least expensive are downtown. Highly recommended lodgings are indicated by a star ★.

Category	Cost*
$$$$	over $160
$$$	$90–$160
$$	$40–$90
$	under $40

All prices are for a standard double room, excluding 10% sales (called IVA) tax.

Ixtapa

★ **Krystal Ixtapa.** This attractive beachfront property is part of a Mexican chain. Home to Christine's, Ixtapa's most popular disco, and Bogart's (*see* Dining, *above*), the Krystal is one of the liveliest spots in town. *Playa Palmar, 40880, tel. 753/3–03–33. 254 rooms and suites with bath. Facilities: 2 restaurants, coffee shop, disco, 2 tennis courts, pool. AE, DC, MC, V. $$$$*

Presidente. This is a beautifully landscaped resort that was among Ixtapa's first beachfront properties. The rooms are divided between colonial-style villas that line winding paths through the grounds and a tower with a glass elevator that provides a sensational view of Ixtapa. Room rates include all meals and beverages. *Playa Palmar, 40880, tel. 753/3–00–18. 401 rooms with bath. Facilities: 3 restaurants, bar, 2 tennis courts, 2 pools, wading pool. AE, DC, MC, V. $$$$*

★ **Westin Ixtapa.** Formerly known as the Camino Real, this is a pyramid-shaped hotel whose rooms (all with private balconies) seem to cascade down the hill to secluded Vista Hermosa beach. It is one of Ixtapa's largest hotels and is noted for excellent service. *Playa Vista Hermosa, Box 91, 40880, tel. 753/3–21–21. 428 rooms with bath. Facilities: 3 restaurants, 2 bars, 4 tennis courts, 3 pools, wading pool. AE, DC, MC, V. $$$$*

Dorado Pacífico. A high rise located on the beach in the center of Ixtapa, this hotel is noted for its spectacular atrium lobby, with fountains and panoramic elevators, and a large pool. The rooms are spacious and very well kept. *Playa Palmar, 40880, tel. 753/3–2025. 285 rooms with bath. Facilities: 3 restaurants, bar, 2 lighted tennis courts, pool. AE, DC, MC, V. $$$*

Posada Real. Smaller and more intimate than most of the other Ixtapa hotels, this colonial-style member of the Best Western chain sits on Palmar Beach, has lots of charm, and offers good value. *Playa Palmar, 40880, tel. 753/3–16–85 or 753/3–17–45. 108 rooms with bath. Facilities: 3 restaurants, 2 bars, disco, 2 pools, wading pool. AE, DC, MC, V. $$*

Zihuatanejo   **La Casa Que Canta.** Resembling a thatched-roof pueblo village, the "House That Sings" is perched on a cliff overlooking La Ropa Beach. All of the individually decorated suites feature ceiling fans as well as air-conditioning, luxurious bathrooms, hand-painted and -crafted furniture, and unique Mexican handicrafts. Two have private pools. The on-premises restaurant is excellent (*see* Chapter 6, Dining). Children under 16 are not accepted. *Camino Escénico a Playa La Ropa, 40880, tel. 753/4–27–22. 18 suites. Facilities: restaurant, pools, beach club. AE, DC, MC, V. $$$$*

Puerto Mío. This small hotel overlooking Zihuatanejo Bay is part of a marina and residential development. The suites, distributed among several Mediterranean-style villas, are tastefully furnished, and the decor makes wonderful use of the bright colors associated with Mexico. *Playa del Almacen, Bahía de Zihuatanejo, 40880, tel. 753/4–37–45, fax 753/4–27–48. 26 suites. Facilities: pool, 2 tennis courts, restaurant, bar. AE, DC, MC, V. $$$$*

★ **Villa del Sol.** A small hotel with a reputation as one of the finest in Mexico, the Villa del Sol is set on the best beach in Zihuatanejo. Although the hotel has all the amenities of a large resort, it retains an intimate feeling. Rates include breakfast and dinner; children under 14 are not accepted in high season. *Playa La Ropa, Box 84, 40880, tel. 753/4–22–39. 59 air-conditioned suites (1 and 2 bedrooms). Facilities: restaurant, pool, beach club, tennis court. AE, MC, V. $$$$*

Irma. Simple and clean, this hotel on a bluff overlooking Playa La Madera (and accessible by a stairway) gets lots of repeat visitors. Guests may use the beach club at the Fiesta Mexicana. *Playa la Madera, Box 4, 40880, tel. 753/4–20–25. 75 rooms with bath. Facilities: restaurant-bar, 2 pools, tennis. AE, DC, MC, V. $$$*

★ **Villas Miramar.** Overlooking La Madera beach, the pretty stucco rooms are nicely decorated and have tiled showers, air-conditioning, and ceiling fans. This all-suite hotel is a good value, but you need to book three months in advance and sometimes as much as two years ahead for Christmas and Easter. *Playa La Madera, Box 211, 40880, tel. 753/4–21–06. 18 suites. Facilities: restaurant, bar. AE, MC, V. $$$*

Avila. Downtown and close to all the pier activity, the Avila has large clean rooms (some are air-conditioned), TVs, and ceiling fans. *Calle Juan N. Alvarez 8, 40880, tel. 753/4–20–10. 27 rooms with bath. AE, MC, V. $$*

Bungalows Pacíficos. Each of these bungalows features two spacious, well-ventilated rooms (sleeping four between them), a kitchen, and a large terrace. *Playa la Madera, 40880, tel. 753/4–21–12. 6 bungalows. No credit cards. $$*

Catalina-Sotovento. Really two hotels in one, this oldie-but-goodie sits on a cliff overlooking the beach, to which you descend on stairs. The rooms are large and decorated in Mexican colonial style, with ceiling fans. All the rooms were recently renovated, and 30 suites with large terraces overlooking the beach were added. *Playa La Ropa, Box 2, 40880, tel. 753/4–20–32 through 42 (10 lines), fax 753/4–29–75. 154 rooms with bath. Facilities: 2 restaurants, 2 bars. AE, DC, MC, V. $$*

Fiesta Mexicana. The pretty Mediterranean-style rooms are surrounded by inviting palm-shaded gardens. Make reservations well in advance, especially for the winter season. *Playa la Ropa, Box 4, 40880, tel. 753/4–37–76. 61 rooms with bath. Facilities: restaurant, bar, pool. AE, DC, MC, V. $$*

Villas las Urracas. Each of the units has a porch in a shaded garden, a kitchen, and a stove. Bungalows las Urracas is a great bargain—and lots of people know it, which places it in great demand. *Playa La Ropa, Box 141, 40880, tel. 753/4–20–49. 16 bungalows. No credit cards. $$*

Casa de la Tortuga. Those seeking seclusion and

inexpensive lodgings in the Ixtapa/Zihuatanejo area might venture some 30 minutes northwest (up the coast) to the tiny village of Trocones. A main house offers clean, simply furnished rooms (two with private baths) with a kitchen and barbecue facilities; the entire house can be rented for a reasonable rate. Farther along the beach is a handful of newly constructed bungalows with queen beds, private baths, and hammocks out front. Services in the area are limited, but the owner is happy to pick up supplies in town for guests. Breakfast is included in the room rates. *Trocones beach, Apdo. 37, Zihuatanejo, Guerrero 40880, tel. and fax 753/4-32-96. 6 rooms, 6 bungalows. Facilities: horseback riding, water sports, restaurant. No credit cards. $*

The Arts and Nightlife

A good way to start an evening is at a happy hour in one of Ixtapa's hotels. Drinks are two for the price of one, and there is no cover charge to enjoy the live music—and, of course, the sunset. **The Bay Club,** on the road to Playa La Ropa, has a marvelous ocean view. **Mariano's** bar in Zihuatanejo is where the locals hang out. The decor is nothing special, but everyone goes, especially singles. **Benji-Pio Bar,** in the El Portal shopping center, and **Le Club,** at the Westin Ixtapa, are also popular. **Christine's** at the Krystal in Ixtapa is the town's liveliest disco. Two discos that attract a spirited young crowd are **Magic Circus** and **Visage.** Both are in the Galerías shopping mall across from the Ixtapa Palace hotel.

Euforia is a spectacular new disco across from the Posada Real hotel. Every night **Carlos 'n' Charlie's** has a dance party on a raised platform on the beach. On Friday night the **Sheraton Ixtapa** and the **Villa del Sol** hotel in Zihuatanejo stage lively Mexican Fiestas that are lots of fun.

There is a movie house with several screens, the **Multicinema Vicente Guerrero,** next to the Somex bank on Calle Vicente Guerrero. Tickets cost about $1.50. Movies in English generally have Spanish subtitles.

Index

Personal Itinerary

Departure *Date*

Time

Transportation

Arrival *Date*   *Time*

Departure *Date*   *Time*

Transportation

Arrival *Date*   *Time*

Departure *Date*   *Time*

Transportation

Arrival *Date*   *Time*

Departure *Date*   *Time*

Transportation

Personal Itinerary

Arrival   *Date*   *Time*

Departure   *Date*   *Time*

Transportation

Arrival   *Date*   *Time*

Departure   *Date*   *Time*

Transportation

Arrival   *Date*   *Time*

Departure   *Date*   *Time*

Transportation

Arrival   *Date*   *Time*

Departure   *Date*   *Time*

Transportation

Addresses

Name	*Name*
Address	*Address*
Telephone	*Telephone*
Name	*Name*
Address	*Address*
Telephone	*Telephone*
Name	*Name*
Address	*Address*
Telephone	*Telephone*
Name	*Name*
Address	*Address*
Telephone	*Telephone*
Name	*Name*
Address	*Address*
Telephone	*Telephone*
Name	*Name*
Address	*Address*
Telephone	*Telephone*
Name	*Name*
Address	*Address*
Telephone	*Telephone*
Name	*Name*
Address	*Address*
Telephone	*Telephone*

*The only guide to explore a
Disney World®️ you've never seen before:*

The one for grown-ups.

0-679-02490-5 $14.00 ($18.50 Can)

This is the only guide written specifically for the millions of adults who visit Walt Disney World®️ each year <u>without</u> kids. Upscale, sophisticated, packed full of facts and maps, *Walt Disney World®️ for Adults* provides up-to-date information on hotels, restaurants, sports facilities, and health clubs, as well as unique itineraries for adults. With *Walt Disney World®️ for Adults* in hand, readers get the most out of one of the world's most fascinating, most complex playgrounds.

At bookstores everywhere, or call **1-800-533-6478.**

Fodor's Travel Guides

Available at bookstores everywhere, or call 1–800–533–6478, 24 hours a day.

U.S. Guides

Alaska

Arizona

Boston

California

Cape Cod, Martha's Vineyard, Nantucket

The Carolinas & the Georgia Coast

Chicago

Colorado

Florida

Hawaii

Las Vegas, Reno, Tahoe

Los Angeles

Maine, Vermont, New Hampshire

Maui

Miami & the Keys

New England

New Orleans

New York City

Pacific North Coast

Philadelphia & the Pennsylvania Dutch Country

The Rockies

San Diego

San Francisco

Santa Fe, Taos, Albuquerque

Seattle & Vancouver

The South

The U.S. & British Virgin Islands

USA

The Upper Great Lakes Region

Virginia & Maryland

Waikiki

Walt Disney World and the Orlando Area

Washington, D.C.

Foreign Guides

Acapulco, Ixtapa, Zihuatanejo

Australia & New Zealand

Austria

The Bahamas

Baja & Mexico's Pacific Coast Resorts

Barbados

Berlin

Bermuda

Brittany & Normandy

Budapest

Canada

Cancún, Cozumel, Yucatán Peninsula

Caribbean

China

Costa Rica, Belize, Guatemala

The Czech Republic & Slovakia

Eastern Europe

Egypt

Euro Disney

Europe

Florence, Tuscany & Umbria

France

Germany

Great Britain

Greece

Hong Kong

India

Ireland

Israel

Italy

Japan

Kenya & Tanzania

Korea

London

Madrid & Barcelona

Mexico

Montréal & Québec City

Morocco

Moscow & St. Petersburg

The Netherlands, Belgium & Luxembourg

New Zealand

Norway

Nova Scotia, Prince Edward Island & New Brunswick

Paris

Portugal

Provence & the Riviera

Rome

Russia & the Baltic Countries

Scandinavia

Scotland

Singapore

South America

Southeast Asia

Spain

Sweden

Switzerland

Thailand

Tokyo

Toronto

Turkey

Vienna & the Danube Valley

Special Series

Fodor's Affordables

Caribbean

Europe

Florida

France

Germany

Great Britain

Italy

London

Paris

Fodor's Bed & Breakfast and Country Inns Guides

America's Best B&Bs

California

Canada's Great Country Inns

Cottages, B&Bs and Country Inns of England and Wales

Mid-Atlantic Region

New England

The Pacific Northwest

The South

The Southwest

The Upper Great Lakes Region

The Berkeley Guides

California

Central America

Eastern Europe

Europe

France

Germany & Austria

Great Britain & Ireland

Italy

London

Mexico

Pacific Northwest & Alaska

Paris

San Francisco

Fodor's Exploring Guides

Australia

Boston & New England

Britain

California

The Caribbean

Florence & Tuscany

Florida

France

Germany

Ireland

Italy

London

Mexico

New York City

Paris

Prague

Rome

Scotland

Singapore & Malaysia

Spain

Thailand

Turkey

Fodor's Flashmaps

Boston

New York

Washington, D.C.

Fodor's Pocket Guides

Acapulco

Bahamas

Barbados

Jamaica

London

New York City

Paris

Puerto Rico

San Francisco

Washington, D.C.

Fodor's Sports

Cycling

Golf Digest's Best Places to Play

Hiking

The Insider's Guide to the Best Canadian Skiing

Running

Sailing

Skiing in the USA & Canada

USA Today's Complete Four Sports Stadium Guide

Fodor's Three-In-Ones (guidebook, language cassette, and phrase book)

France

Germany

Italy

Mexico

Spain

Fodor's Special-Interest Guides

Complete Guide to America's National Parks

Condé Nast Traveler Caribbean Resort and Cruise Ship Finder

Cruises and Ports of Call

Euro Disney

France by Train

Halliday's New England Food Explorer

Healthy Escapes

Italy by Train

London Companion

Shadow Traffic's New York Shortcuts and Traffic Tips

Sunday in New York

Sunday in San Francisco

Touring Europe

Touring USA: Eastern Edition

Walt Disney World and the Orlando Area

Walt Disney World for Adults

Fodor's Vacation Planners

Great American Learning Vacations

Great American Sports & Adventure Vacations

Great American Vacations

Great American Vacations for Travelers with Disabilities

National Parks and Seashores of the East

National Parks of the West

The Wall Street Journal Guides to Business Travel

At last — a guide for Americans with disabilities that makes traveling a delight

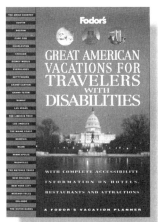

0-679-02591-X $18.00 ($24.00 Can)

This is the first and only complete guide to great American vacations for the 35 million North Americans with disabilities, as well as for those who care for them or for aging parents and relatives. Provides:

• Essential trip-planning information for travelers with mobility, vision, and hearing impairments

• Specific details on a huge array of facilities, along with solid descriptions of attractions, hotels, restaurants, and other destinations

• Up-to-date information on ISA-designated parking, level entranceways, and accessibility to pools, lounges, and bathrooms